Being Brown

AMERICAN STUDIES NOW:
CRITICAL HISTORIES OF THE PRESENT

Edited by Lisa Duggan and Curtis Marez

Much of the most exciting contemporary work in American Studies refuses the distinction between politics and culture, focusing on historical cultures of power and protest on the one hand, or the political meanings and consequences of cultural practices, on the other. American Studies Now offers concise, accessible, authoritative books on significant political debates, personalities, and popular cultural phenomena quickly, while such teachable moments are at the forefront of public consciousness.

1. *We Demand: The University and Student Protests,* by Roderick A. Ferguson

2. *The Fifty-Year Rebellion: How the U.S. Political Crisis Began in Detroit,* by Scott Kurashige

3. *Trans*: A Quick and Quirky Account of Gender Variability,* by Jack Halberstam

4. *Boycott! The Academy and Justice for Palestine,* by Sunaina Maira

5. *Imagining the Future of Climate Change: World-Making through Science Fiction and Activism,* by Shelley Streeby

6. *Making All Black Lives Matter: Reimagining Freedom in the Twenty-First Century,* by Barbara Ransby

7. *Beyond the Pink Tide: Art and Political Undercurrents in the Americas,* by Macarena Gómez-Barris

8. *Mean Girl: Ayn Rand and the Culture of Greed,* by Lisa Duggan

9. *Being Brown: Sonia Sotomayor and the Latino Question,* by Lázaro Lima

Being Brown

*Sonia Sotomayor and
the Latino Question*

Lázaro Lima

UNIVERSITY OF CALIFORNIA PRESS

*The publisher and the University of California Press Foundation
gratefully acknowledge the generous support of the Anne G. Lipow
Fund in Social Justice and Human Rights.*

University of California Press
Oakland, California

Library of Congress Cataloging-in-Publication Data
Names: Lima, Lázaro, author.
Title: Being brown : Sonia Sotomayor and the Latino
    question / Lázaro Lima.
Description: Oakland, California : University of
    California Press, [2019] |Includes bibliographical
    references. |
Identifiers: LCCN 2019019375 (print) | LCCN 2019021813
    (ebook) | ISBN 9780520972087 (ebook and ePDF) |
    ISBN 9780520300880 (cloth : alk. paper) |
    ISBN 9780520300897 (pbk. : alk. paper)
Subjects: LCSH: Sotomayor, Sonia, 1954– | Judges—
    United States—Biography. |Hispanic American
    judges—Biography.
Classification: LCC KF8745.S67 (ebook) | LCC KF8745.S67
    L56 2020 (print) | DDC 347.73/2634—dc23
LC record available at https://lccn.loc.gov/2019019375

For Christina Valera, Liska Gutiérrez,
and Alex Gutiérrez

CONTENTS

Overview ix

Introduction. On Being Brown
in the Democratic Commons

I

PART I. A LATINA FOR THE NATION

1. Sonia Sotomayor and "the Latino Question"

17

2. Sonia Sotomayor's Elusive Embrace

45

PART II. LOSING SONIA SOTOMAYOR

3. Sonia Sotomayor, the Mediapheme

81

4. Sonia Sotomayor and Other States of Debt
122

Coda. Thinking Otherwise: Sonia Sotomayor and
the Emergence of Latino Legal Thought
150

Acknowledgments 173

Notes 177

Selected Bibliography 195

OVERVIEW

INTRODUCTION. ON BEING BROWN
IN THE DEMOCRATIC COMMONS

Latinos are the largest minority group in the United States but the most disenfranchised from American institutions. Sonia Sotomayor is the first Latina on the Supreme Court, and that represents progress to some, but it comes at the price of historical amnesia. Ignoring that the legally mandated forms of inclusion that facilitated her ascent to the court no longer exist creates a false sense of political enfranchisement that doesn't yet exist for Latinos.

Being Brown · *Supreme Court* · *Black and Brown Lives* · *Democratic Commons* · *Historical Amnesia*

PART I. A LATINA FOR THE NATION

CHAPTER 1. SONIA SOTOMAYOR AND "THE LATINO QUESTION"

Answering "the Latino question"—What is the country to do with Latinos, and what are Latinos to do about their disenfranchisement from American civic life?—requires a confrontation with Trumpism's assault on the civil rights of

minorities and Latinos in particular. While the 1954
Supreme Court case *Hernández v. Texas* constitutionally
mandated Fourteenth Amendment protections for Latinos,
it has been largely ignored. The case needs to be reconsid-
ered for the protections it may provide.

"The Latino Question" · *Hernández v. Texas* ·
"The Negro Problem" · *"The Jewish Question"* · *The Brown Commons*

CHAPTER 2. SONIA SOTOMAYOR'S
ELUSIVE EMBRACE

Sotomayor's significant educational achievements were
made possible by sheer determination and "affirmative
action." By the time she graduated from law school in 1979,
however, the *Regents of the University of California v. Bakke*
(1978) decision had already stacked the deck against affirmative action. Less than fourteen years after the passage of the
Civil Rights Act of 1964, the *Bakke* case eliminated the
quota-driven forms of redress that allowed minorities access
to social mobility through education.

University of California v. Bakke · *Affirmative Action* ·
Civil Rights Act · *Multiculturalism*

PART II. LOSING SONIA SOTOMAYOR

CHAPTER 3. SONIA SOTOMAYOR,
THE MEDIAPHEME

The use value of Sotomayor's life story was read differently
by various national constituencies depending on their
political goals. The rise of new media coincided with her
ascent to the court, as did the rise of "alternative facts." A
"mediapheme" encapsulates the most resonant, but not the
most truthful or accurate, version of a person, story, or event
that travels through channels of mass communication
susceptible to "deepfake": false representations of real
events. Thus the mediapheme, unchecked or uncountered,
creates "truthiness" and can destabilize democratic processes that rely on facts. Newt Gingrich's Contract with
America ushered in an assault on "expertise" and created

the scaffolding for rolling back civil rights victories, diminishing democratic checks and balances, and the eventual disrespect for evidence that we have inherited in today's political culture.

Mediapheme · "Deepfake" · "Alternative Facts" ·
Fake News · Democratic Checks and Balances ·
Newt Gingrich · Contract with America

CHAPTER 4. SONIA SOTOMAYOR AND OTHER STATES OF DEBT

Sotomayor was the most financially indebted justice to arrive on the court. She was also indebted to the first Black president for nominating her, as well as to her parents, whose personal sacrifice led them to New York City in search of a better life. The most significant debts, however, were erased in the telling of her success story and included the hidden history of U.S. empire building in Puerto Rico and related biological experiments on Puerto Ricans. These experiments led to the sterilization of over a third of all women on the island and the torture of political prisoners. It also led Nationalists like Pedro Albizu Campos, Dolores "Lolita" Lebrón Sotomayor, and many others to resist the U.S. sacking of the island and its people.

Odious Debt · Celina Báez · Juan Luis Sotomayor ·
Puerto Rican Nationalists · Pedro Albizu Campos ·
Lolita Lebrón · Sterilization · Eugenics · Puerto Rican Independence
Movement · Extractive Capitalism

CODA. THINKING OTHERWISE: SONIA SOTOMAYOR AND THE EMERGENCE OF LATINO LEGAL THOUGHT

While on the Second Circuit Court of Appeals from 1998 to 2009, Sotomayor had a jurisprudential record that aligned her with conservative causes and outcomes. There was a transformation in her jurisprudential thinking after she arrived on the Supreme Court. She used the term *undocumented immigrant* for the first time in the history of the Supreme Court (against *illegal alien*) and became a defender of due process protections, Fourteenth Amendment protections, and LGBTQ rights. Sotomayor's "thinking otherwise" might be paving the way for the emergence of "Latino legal thought" and the instantiation of greater equity under the law.

Critical Race Theory · LatCrit · LGBTQ Rights · Latino Legal Thought · "Thinking Otherwise"

Introduction

On Being Brown in the Democratic Commons

> When a young person, even a gifted one, grows up
> without proximate living examples of what she may
> aspire to become—whether lawyer, scientist, artist or
> leader in any realm—her goal remains abstract....
> A role model in the flesh provides more than inspiration;
> his or her very existence is confirmation of possibilities
> one may have every reason to doubt, saying, "Yes,
> someone like me can do this."
>
> Sonia Sotomayor[1]

Sonia Sotomayor's nomination and eventual confirmation to the Supreme Court proved to be momentous for the country and of profound cultural and historical significance to Latinos.[2] This is because Latinos—peoples of Latin American origin or ancestry living in the United States—have the distinction of being both the nation's largest minority, at over 57.5 million strong, and the most disenfranchised from American institutions and circuits of political power.[3] Not surprisingly, Sotomayor's story of accomplishment and her eventual rise to the pinnacle of American public life seemed to herald an important transformation that augured well for the legitimation and incorporation of Latinos into the fiber of American civic institutions. Supreme Court confirmations have traditionally served as bellwethers of either significant cultural change or the static perpetuation of the political status quo for the nation. Just as Justices Louis Brandeis (1856–1941), Thurgood Marshall (1908–93), and Sandra Day O'Connor (1930–) marked and signaled the greater acceptance of Jewish Americans, African Americans, and women into the country's circuits of power through their incorporation into one of its foundational institutions, Sotomayor's confirmation on August 6, 2009, represented the fulfillment of a promise of equality of access to opportunity that underwrites the American dream. Astonishingly, and for the first time in the history of the country, Latinos had proof that despite their over five-hundred-year presence in what is now the United States,[4] they were at last part of the nation's official cultural history with a representative Latina who had a seat at the table on the Supreme Court. Sotomayor's entry into the hallowed halls of justice ultimately represented what by most accounts was a massive blow to a history of Latino disenfranchisement from the existing political and racial order, and—not inconsequentially—it signaled an important shift in the way the national culture understands the country's largest minority. In the process, Sotomayor has become "a role model in the flesh," or what I am here calling "a representative Latina."[5] Yet given the profound changes occasioned by the demographic reality of a new Latino "majority minority" to the nation's founding traditions, cultural history, common language, institutions, and national character, can Sotomayor's story inspire hope for Latinos and other disenfranchised communities, as well as quell the fears of a majority culture ill equipped to understand its largest majority-minority group?

This book considers Sotomayor's life story to be revelatory and central to understanding what I am here provocatively calling "the Latino question": What is the country to do with its most disenfranchised and misunderstood "majority minority"? And, conversely, what are Latinos to do about their disenfranchisement from American civic life? *Being Brown: Sonia Sotomayor and the Latino Question* tells the story of Sotomayor's formidable rise from poverty and her journey to the Supreme Court as an opportunity to reflect on the complexity of the country's relationship to Latinos at a moment of profound demographic, economic, social, and political upheaval. It is not a conventional biography in that it asks us to consider how Sotomayor's life story can be read in relation to the Latino question at a critical moment of both opportunity and guarded apprehension for Latinos, as well as for the country. *Being Brown* is fundamentally shaped by my interest in understanding what Sotomayor's improbable rise from poverty can tell us about our country's relationship to Latinos and their cultural history, and what we stand to gain or lose by understanding her spectacular story of ascent as a representative Latina for the nation. The need to understand the current historical moment of heretofore unthinkable "blood and soil" Nazism, of blatant racism at the highest levels of government against Latinos, and of politically disenfranchised cultural others, along with media-induced "alternative realities," makes a historical accounting all the more necessary. As we shall see, if in the process I am critical of the use value of Sotomayor's uplifting story and its representativeness to the broader Latino question, I do so only because the evidence I interpret herein requires critical distance from the overwhelming and uncritical adulation that her narrative has received.

In *Being Brown,* I contend that we ultimately perform a disservice to democracy, and its attendant promise of equality of access and egalitarian inclusion for all, when we allow biographies of uplift, however compelling, necessary, and alluring they may be, to substitute for the political work of inclusion that democratic practice and civic responsibility demand. I also contend that celebrating a public figure's attributes as a representative of group identity too often runs the risk of actually leaving in place the very forms exclusion that such symbolic representation seeks to remedy. In the process, *Being Brown* also tells the story of what we stand to lose as a country if we continue to sleepwalk through history by allowing stories of inclusion and social mobility to sedate us to the lived realities and the daunting collective work that democratic inclusion truly demands at this pressing historical juncture characterized by crisis and media spectacles. Imagining just what that daunting collective work of liberation might look like, and moving toward its enactment, may require that we lose Sonia Sotomayor. Not the person, of course, or—as we shall see—the exceptional life story that has already helped inspire such a task, but the exhausted recourse to an exemplary biography that promises inclusion but paradoxically erases the necessary historical accounting that might make such inclusion possible. That accounting requires that we eschew the ever-seductive but always elusive embrace of symbolic inclusion in order to imaginatively instantiate democracy's ever-regenerative promise of social equity and equality of access. Doing so requires an understanding of "being Brown" as both a state of being and a relational identity within the state of U.S. political culture.

BEING BROWN

I am interested in a mode of affective particularity
that I am describing as brownness, and this focus
leads me to the project of describing particular

performances of brown feelings that produce
knowledge about singularities and pluralities that do
not conform to anticipatable notions of reason.
    José Esteban Muñoz[6]

José Esteban Muñoz (1967–2013) described "brownness" as a *being* in the world marked by epistemological invisibility. Muñoz's project was decidedly philosophical in its attempt to make visible how certain forms of *being* and *knowing* by cultural others are erased when those ways of being and knowing are marked as "unreasonable." His work called for a rethinking of "philosophical universalism" and its insistence on a universal ethic that applies to all people regardless of racial, sexual, cultural, gendered, or other human differences. Accounting for how certain ways of being and knowing fall outside the strictures of philosophical universalism required generative framing questions. What types of knowing and being are excluded from analytical engagement and meaningful world making? What ways of being in the world are erased when we presume certain forms of knowledge to be unworthy of philosophical interrogation and investigation? Muñoz called this process of unlearning philosophical universalism "thinking otherwise," and phenomenology provided an entry point for understanding the "Brown democratic commons" as a space for participation unhampered by normative forms of legal and epistemic violence that delimit and demean "other" ways of being in the world. Muñoz explained his purpose plaintively in an early essay in which he intended "to enable a project that imagines a position or narrative of being and becoming that can resist the pull of identitarian models of relationality."[7] His engagement with continental philosophy was nothing short of daunting insofar as it required breaking universalism's "ecumenical standard"—a universalizing standard or measure that ignores ethnic, racial, or other differences—in order to imagine ways of being and knowing that would allow people to understand how epistemic or state-sanctioned violence differently affects cultural others.

Universalists consider identity politics counter to reasonable philosophical inquiry because "identitarians"—those who stress their social situatedness as "Latinx," "African American," "queer," and so on, beyond their common humanity—are purportedly too beholden to their social estrangement to the detriment of their participation in the broader democratic commons. While there is much to learn from analytically distancing ourselves from our social situatedness, such a universalist response to difference runs the risk of assuming that we all have equal access to social agency, irrespective of our differences. Universalists seem to forget that while, for example, getting hit over the head with a baseball bat hurts everyone similarly, regardless of whether you are a white man or an African American teenager, it is the bodies of Black and Brown cultural others who bear the brutal brunt of such violence. The literal and epistemic violence against cultural others manifests itself in the unequal application of the law, which belies the purported "equal treatment under the law" that universalists presume a priori. That the Black Lives Matter movement has endeavored so assiduously to make this commonplace visible should reveal the ecumenical standard for the fiction that it is.[8] That is to say, a universalist call for an "ecumenical standard" across differences erases the very violence and the necessary accounting that would make "equality for all" meaningful in the democratic commons. The democratic commons, that space of messy self-governance in the unruly town square, is under assault, and such a value-neutral position in the face of unparalleled racism, ethnonationalism, and xenophobia should be considered ethically untenable and met with resistance. Muñoz walked that fine line between materialism and idealism in order to instantiate in the world a *being* that is responsive to differences but not beholden to them, thereby mapping the exigencies of what in the future might be a democratic commons inflected with "a sense of brown."

The book Muñoz was completing before his untimely death, *Sense of Brown,* would have undoubtedly provided a theoretical anchor to *Being Brown.*[9] While Muñoz was concerned with finding a phenomenological way out of this "identitarian" impasse, my purpose here is far more modest. In grounding my project in materially related relations of cause and effect, I situate "brownness" vis-à-vis the Latino question. I do this for two principal reasons: first, to demand an accounting that would render the Latino body legible within the national body politic and, second, to foreground a conversation about how fortifying the democratic commons necessarily requires Latino political emergence and participation. In this project, I propose that being Brown should be understood primarily, though certainly not exclusively, as a relation to the state, something that would have been too myopic for Muñoz's expansive philosophical enterprise. I do so because unless we make the Brown commons visible, and the state responsible for responding to the exigencies that the Latino question requires, we will continually run the risk of social invisibility and continued political disenfranchisement. *Being Brown* therefore insists on foregrounding the discourses of law, media studies, and cultural representation as the most propitious lenses through which to understand the dynamics of being Brown in the United States at this historical juncture. It is therefore in this spirit of visibility and accountability that *Being Brown* seeks to provide an archive of minoritarian resistance, as well as a potential method for creative world making in the face of historical erasures, through a shared vocabulary of facts that takes the Latino question to task. Latino agency is and has been central to the democratic commons, and this book is another example of Brown agency as democratic *doing*.

ENGAGING THE LATINO QUESTION

Opening with this introduction and closing with a coda, *Being Brown* is divided into two parts. A separate and accompanying web page archives images and resources, and expands the utility and purpose of the book to readers (https://www.lazarolima.com/being-brown.html). In the chapters that follow, I provide a combination of historical context for Sotomayor's life story and critical analysis of the processes through which she has become the most visible representative Latino figure in the nation, as well as the costs that such a representative character enacts on the American body politic when the use value of a media image substitutes the work of historical and political accounting that our moment demands and her significant life story requires. This is particularly urgent when we consider not only that Latinos have been historically disenfranchised from American civic institutions but also that they are currently the most discriminated-against national minority, even to the point of being considered "racially" inferior in "respectable" public discourse. Even though Latinos do not constitute a "race," since they can comprise a gamut of racial and ethnic configurations, and even though race is a specious category devoid of analytical validity, pundits have gone so far as to suggest that Latinos are a national imposition *because* they are genetically inferior. If this seems like an exaggeration, the following chapters will both document and illustrate otherwise by foregrounding the exigencies of the Latino question.

Part I, "A Latina for the Nation," analyzes Sotomayor's story of success in the context of rising anti-Latino sentiment and the neoliberal gutting of education. Chapter 1 traces how anti-Latino sentiment emerged before and during Sotomayor's ascent to the Supreme Court, as well as how "science" is being weaponized against the Latino body politic. The chapter also engages the legacy of the civil rights era and how a little-known Supreme Court case, *Hernández v. Texas* (1954), extended Fourteenth Amendment protections to Latinos, as well as how the histories of Latino jurisprudence might help bring us closer to democratic enfranchisement. In chapter 2, the "American dream" is analyzed in relation to the stories of social mobility through education that make it more implausible than ever after the gutting of public education. As the critic Tavia Nyong'o has reminded us, the American dream is a Janus-faced trope "that demands that the U.S. remain the object of the other's desire," and this chapter elaborates that which the American dream narrative obviates through violent erasures.[10]

Part II, "Losing Sonia Sotomayor," frames how the end of expertise and the rise of "alternative facts" threaten democratic practice by evacuating history from the national consciousness. Chapter 3 puts into dialogue the spectacular versions of Sotomayor's story of success and how various constituencies used that story to wildly different ends. The chapter further explains how historically driven relations of cause and effect have given way to the rise of "alternative facts" in the current "bread and circuses" regime of the day. Chapter 4 brings into focus the story of Sotomayor's parents' migration within the broader history of U.S.–Puerto Rican relations and the legacies of American empire building in the Caribbean. It provides the necessary groundwork for understanding how the Puerto Rican diaspora in the United

States still remains regrettably underanalyzed yet key to understanding whether Sotomayor's life story is in fact representative of the various national Latino communities that she is made to represent. The chapter also necessarily engages the question of debt and indebtedness in a political moment of austerity and profound economic transformations. Neoliberal austerity, the reigning economic paradigm, posits that spending less, refusing to forgive debt, and shrinking government is the solution to a persistent economic crisis; it here serves as a useful analogue to Sotomayor's story of indebtedness to familial sacrifice and the broader largesse of the nation she credits with her success.

DEMOCRACY'S HEIRS

Being Brown ultimately underscores and puts into dialogue key events from Sotomayor's biography and their relationship to significant debates in U.S. cultural history about the nature of Latino belonging, Latin American immigration and migration, the politics of civic participation for racialized minorities, and the virtually unknown history of U.S.–Puerto Rico relations in public culture. Sotomayor stands among the most recognizable Latino figures in the nation, and she has already received considerable notoriety for broadening the discussion about the Latino question. But as a representative Latina, she has also been the subject of timeworn "Latin" stereotypes in the media about the nature of legality and national belonging, as well as newer, more complex mythologies. The latter attempt to divorce her public success from the necessary personal, sexual, historical, and affective life that should be integrated into the broader public story about this remarkable human being who identifies as a Latina.

The separation of the personal from the public, the sensual from the political, is insidious in its ability to trap important stories into an impossible Manichean duality of either a "good" or "bad" ethnic subject, a duality that delimits agency for both the real person and those who stand to learn from her.

Given the complexity of Sotomayor's story, its relevance and valence to various constituencies, I have made an effort to draw on a variety of materials that include archival sources, newspapers, television reports, talk radio, oral interviews, speeches, correspondence, and digital and social media. The versions of Sotomayor's Latina life story that circulate in and through mass media, in respected outlets as well as the less regulated terrain of Twitter and the blogosphere, ultimately help construct and produce knowledge—wittingly or not, disinterestedly or not—about the nature of belonging, and they shape the national discussion on who should matter, and who should not, within the broader national body politic. Indeed, at no other time in history have digital media played such an important role in the creation of a representative Latina for the nation who can move so effortlessly across generational, economic, racial, class, linguistic, and gendered registers. Focusing on diverse media also allows us to investigate how new forms of technology also produce new kinds of political spaces and subjects, as well as how the internet both conditions and delimits these social spaces of emergence and contestation, while paradoxically creating and speeding this process. The arrival of these new technologies that circulate knowledge with unimaginable speed, and without accountability, have fundamentally altered our ability to parse truth from fiction, and Sotomayor's arrival on the national scene coincides with this phenomenon broadly known as "deepfake."

The term *deepfake,* combined from *deep learning* and *fake news,* refers to technologies that emerged from a 2018 desktop application called FakeApp, which allows users to share videos with faces swapped. After the 2016 election, when the presidency of the world's most powerful nation was purported to have been undermined by Russian interference, it becomes ever more necessary to understand and name phenomena that can alter perception and political culture in ways that were previously unimaginable and that are antithetical to democratic practice.

It is in this context that it becomes particularly important at this historical moment to be explicit about the limits of inclusion and education as the means through which to achieve social mobility when the systemic and ideological structures that purportedly establish equality of access have frustrated rather than facilitated upward mobility and political enfranchisement. Ultimately, the goal of the book is to understand Sotomayor's rise in prominence in order to engage in a broader national conversation, with respect and clarity, for the complexities that the Latino question raises in relation to her role as a representative Latina for the nation. As Latinos and as Americans, we should honor and recognize how exemplary stories such as Sotomayor's can give us the courage to imagine and even invent more equitable and democratic futures, provided we learn to distinguish between inclusion's ever-elusive and perennially deferred embrace and the actual instantiation and political enactment of lived equality of access, which is required for the flourishing of robust democratic practice through *doing.* I contend in what follows that only then can we, as democracy's aspirants, become democracy's heirs. *Being Brown* constitutes an attempt at deciphering what is still a larger and misunderstood history of Latinos' relationship to national identity, inequality, race, resistance, and power relations in contemporary American political culture through its most representative and public Latino figure in the country, Sonia Sotomayor. Such an understanding is crucial now more than ever as the nation struggles to understand its constitutive identify and the role of the Latino body politic in its potential futures.

PART I

A Latina for the Nation

Optimism is cruel when the object/scene that ignites a sense of possibility actually makes it impossible to attain the expansive transformation for which a person or a people risks a striving.

Lauren Berlant, *Cruel Optimism* (2011)

CHAPTER ONE

Sonia Sotomayor and "the Latino Question"

They approach me in a half-hesitant sort of way, eye
me curiously or compassionately, and then, instead of
saying directly, How does it feel to be a problem? they
say, I know an excellent colored man in my town.

W. E. B. Du Bois[1]

What is the country to do with its most disenfranchised and
misunderstood "majority minority," and what are Latinos to do
about their disenfranchisement from "American" civic life?
What I am here referring to as "the Latino question" is meant to
draw attention to two of its historical parallels, "the Jewish question" and "the Negro problem." Much as "the Jewish question"
comprised a debate about the status and appropriate treatment
of Jews in Europe during the nineteenth and twentieth centuries, "the Negro problem" for W. E. B. Du Bois functioned as a
provocative shorthand that allowed him to critically engage how
Black agency confronted white supremacy as formerly enslaved
peoples sought entry into American civic life after the Civil
War (1861–65). For Du Bois, "the Negro problem" called attention both to how the history of slavery paradoxically made

whites incapable of seeing their role as progenitors of the very problem they had created, and to how the education of Blacks, certainly, but also of whites, would serve to ameliorate the "problem." When in *The Souls of Black Folks* (1903) Du Bois avers, "How does it feel to be a problem?" he is rhetorically laying bare how he, and by extension all Blacks, are continually being asked to justify their very existence. While Du Bois's answer to "the problem" in his essay "The Talented Tenth" was that an educated Black elite would go on to be leaders and exemplars of "the race," my interest here is decidedly not prescriptive. Instead, I'd like "the Latino question" to serve as critical shorthand for the Latino conundrum that Sonia Sotomayor has inherited as the nation's best-known and most politically influential Latina. I do so because Sotomayor's life story as a representative Latina, and its use value to the nation, reveals the historically fraught relationship between Latinos and the broader national body politic, as well as the limited circuits of political representation and cultural enfranchisement available to the country's largest "majority minority." As such, Sotomayor's trajectory can illuminate the vagaries of the Latino question.

The Latino question itself is intimately tied to a series of national misapprehensions about the nature of Latinos and their role in American civic life: who they are, where they come from, why they come, and what they purportedly believe, as well as why they are presumed to be recent interlopers in the United States despite their long though unacknowledged history in the country. Indeed, the cultural anxieties surrounding the exigencies brought about by the Latino question have also inaugurated one of the most xenophobic chapters in the country's history and fueled anti-Latino sentiment and rampant discrimination. Even before the arrival of President Donald Trump's unabashed

signature racism, and the concomitant rise of previously unimaginable racist-inflected xenophobia, scholars attempted to
account for the structural divestment of Latinos from American
civic life. The social anthropologist Leo R. Chávez considers
the national misapprehensions surrounding the Latino question
to be at the heart of this divestment, misapprehensions that are
attributable to what he calls "the Latino threat narrative."

Chávez identifies four principal "threat narratives" that both
fuel systemic discrimination against Latinos and prevent an
honest and historically grounded discussion of the Latino question. According to Chávez, the Latino threat narrative purports
"that Latinos do not want to speak English; that Latinos do not
want to integrate socially and culturally into the larger U.S.
society; that the Mexican-origin population, in particular, is
part of a grand conspiracy to take over the U.S. Southwest (the
Reconquista'); and, finally, that 'Latin' women are unable to control their reproductive capacities."[2] Read in relation to the Latino threat narrative, the use value of Sotomayor's story and her
image in the public sphere would seem to counter and assuage
the misconceptions and unfounded fears attributed to the threat
Latinos ostensibly pose to the country. Sotomayor is, after all,
an accomplished Ivy League graduate who has interpreted the
language and spirit of the law for her entire adult life. She has
integrated and embraced the American dream of inclusion and
social mobility as its principal and most visible representative
Latino in the political sphere; she has been duly entrusted to
safeguard the nation's laws as a keeper of the Constitution; and,
not long after her confirmation in 2009, she took it upon herself
to inspire the nation's young—especially Latino and Black
youth—to respect the rule of law and appreciate how civics can
bring us together as Americans. What is more, without having

children herself, she has become a childless mother figure to disenfranchised youth throughout the country. But if Sotomayor's own narrative functions as a counterweight to the fears the Latino threat narrative poses to majority culture, just what are the costs associated with our need to assuage the misapprehensions and related national anxieties brought about by the Latino question through her remarkable story as an American and as a representative Latina? I consider this question to be of pressing significance for our moment.

Imani Perry has parsed the assumptions that subtend the spectacular narratives of minority uplift that inhere to both Sotomayor's and former president Barack Obama's stories of accomplishment in the face of insurmountable odds, narratives that are so stridently appealing for our moment because they reinterpret the story of minority failure to succeed in the national field of signification. They do so by positing exceptional figures that obscure both majoritarian and institutional culpability for the disenfranchisement of so many nationals by making "success" intelligible through the language of "the bootstraps narrative." The language of "the bootstraps" obviates historical accounting for the benefit of a more palatable and easy commonplace: if Obama and Sotomayor can do it, so can every other Black, Latino, or disenfranchised American.[3] The danger, as Perry sees it, and as I echo here, is that these stories of advancement and success run the risk of ultimately depoliticizing the economic and the policy-driven initiatives that could make such minoritarian success possible. That is, we begin to confuse, if not altogether substitute, the trappings of our cultural moment's stories of minority success for the politics of an as-yet-unaccountable state and its vexed relationship to those minorities, as well as the conditions that would make such stories of inclusion meaningful. This is not to suggest, as Perry makes clear, that policies such as affirmative action can put an end to the structural and institutional divestment that such a large swath of our country's population has inherited. Quite the contrary. It is to say that while affirmative action represents the starting point for the legal recognition of broader structural problems, it has also been largely understood as a "giveaway" to those who do not necessarily deserve it. In the process of arriving and breaking glass ceilings through policies that sought to remedy structural inequalities in education, the likes of Obama and Sotomayor inherit a conundrum. They must distance themselves from the commonplace assertions that they may have been undeserving recipients of the nation's greater largesse and in the process reaffirm the "bootstraps narrative," which obviates the need to remember, recount, and reconsider why affirmative action policies were necessary in the first place—not to mention the costs associated with erasing their personal histories for a seat at the table.

Such an uncritical invocation of the bootstraps narrative in our moment ultimately runs the risk of forgetting President Lyndon B. Johnson's important distinction between "equality" and "justice," which he made in his now famous commencement address at Howard University (1965):

> You do not wipe away the scars of centuries by saying: Now you are free to go where you want, and do as you desire, and choose the leaders you please. You do not take a person who, for years, has been hobbled by chains and liberate him, bring him up to the starting line of a race and then say, "you are free to compete with all the others," and still justly believe that you have been completely fair.[4]

We have forgotten Johnson's call to both remember the legacies of exclusion that devalue democratic principles, not to mention people, and to abolish these exclusions as a starting point for fortifying democratic practice. The historical amnesias that bind us to the narratives of bootstraps ultimately forestall the possibility for a national accounting that would make these stories of success and advancement ethically just and democratically meaningful. This is especially true in a historical moment of unrelenting attacks on Latino life and Latinos' very humanity. If that seems like an exaggeration, let us turn to the evidence at hand, first by foregrounding the laws that have specifically targeted Latino populations in an attempt to disenfranchise them and remand them to the edges of democracy's graveyard and, second, by framing how pseudoscience has attempted to provide the scaffolding for the conditions under which Latinos can be deemed less than human.

CITIZENS WITHOUT CITIZENSHIP OR REPRESENTATION: THE TURN TOWARD HISTORICAL AMNESIA

High-concentration Latino-heritage states like Texas and Arizona have institutionalized de facto discrimination against Latinos. One of the most publicized and acrimonious early assaults in this troubling national trend occurred in Texas in 2010, when the state's curriculum committee made significant changes to the Texas's history and social studies requirements at the expense of minorities. Texas textbooks have been a source of consternation for educators nationwide for at least two reasons. First, Texas is one of the largest buyers of textbooks, and the impact of those books and the national pedagogies they instantiate have considerable reach. Second, the state's Board of Education in 2010 approved a "social studies" curriculum that elided historical cause-effect relations by ascribing "conservative values" and exalting Republican Party ideology at the expense of history proper. For example, by the time the Texas textbooks were published and became part of the statewide curriculum in 2015, they had passages stating that Moses—from the Book of Exodus—influenced the writing of the U.S. Constitution. Additionally, these state-sanctioned textbooks juxtaposed Abraham Lincoln's inaugural address with that of Confederate president Jefferson Davis, and they made no mention, as they previously had, of the Supreme Court's first Black justice, Thurgood Marshall, or Mexican American labor leader and Latino civil rights icon César Chávez. Despite protestations from educators and parents alike, the committee rejected calls to include more Latino peoples in the state's education curriculum, even though the state has a large Mexican American population.[5] The historical whitewashing instantiated in 2010 and made respectable by its appearing in schoolbooks can be understood as a broader attempt at creating national pedagogies that inculcate in students a version of a national past devoid of Latino and Black agency. Indeed, from the distance, 2010 appears to have been a signal year for the collective disenfranchisement of Blacks and Latinos from the national imaginary, that is, the storehouse of images and stories the country tells itself about its past, in order to understand its present and its futures. Let us quickly gloss how anti-immigrant initiatives also made their way into state laws and statutes.

In Arizona the passage of the state's Senate Bill 1070 on April 3, 2010, gave local law enforcement the authority to detain citizens and cultural citizens alike without due process if they appear "illegal." Among SB 1070's many controversial provisions, it institutionalized de facto racial profiling by allowing law enforcement officials to question anyone deemed "reasonably suspicious" of being a "noncitizen." Though in June 2012 the Supreme Court struck down most of what came to be known as Arizona's "driving while Brown law" and the "show me your papers law," it still kept intact the provision that allowed law enforcement officials to ask "anyone suspected of being in the country illegally for their immigration papers" or face incarceration. Laws modeled on Arizona's SB 1070 have now been enacted in Alabama, Georgia, Indiana, Mississippi, South Carolina, Utah, and Virginia, and copycat legislation is awaiting review in many other states. Additionally, other legal initiatives to delegitimize knowledge projects critical of white supremacy have also taken root in Arizona, yet another state with a high Latino population.

In 2010, Arizona's House Bill 2281—known as the "anti–ethnic studies law"—further increased the state's control over the Latino body by allowing the state to police knowledge production. The law was directed specifically against an experimental Tucson curriculum for elementary, middle, and high school students that emphasized critical thinking and had a focus on Mexican American and Latino cultural and literary history. The law made it "illegal" to "promote resentment toward a race or class of people," to allow classes that are designed primarily for pupils of a particular ethnic group, or to advocate ethnic solidarity.[6] That the law was passed despite increased graduation rates for Latinos who were reaching graduation parity with Anglo-American students is emblematic of the extent of the state's reach and willingness to delimit Latino social mobility by thwarting educational equity through punitive laws. In other words, Arizona's HB 2281 understood Latino knowledge production and dissemination as an assault on national identity, breeding division, separatism, and conflict, rather than as a largely unsuccessful multicultural attempt at remedying preexisting structural inequalities perpetuated in and through national pedagogies of exclusion. Confounding culture with the politics of the state, Arizona's HB 2281 simply made what it understood to be Latino historical representation and pride the enemy of the state. This despite lawsuits challenging Arizona's HB 2281 that pointed to empirical evidence of increased Latino graduation rates. When the case reached the Supreme Court, most provisions of the anti–ethnic studies law were upheld. What possible consequences can emerge to trouble democratic practice under such circumstances?

Most recently, "denaturalization," the process through which citizens can be legally stripped of their citizenship and due process rights, has emerged in the Trump administration's arsenal against Brown people. Denaturalization is "legal" and can occur against an individual in either civil or criminal proceedings. To prevail against a citizen, the government must either prove that the person in question was never statutorily eligible for citizenship in the first place, or that the person obtained their citizenship by concealing or omitting, wittingly or not, a material fact. Writing in the *Nation,* Rafia Zakaria makes explicit the stakes involved:

> The Trump administration's push to pursue denaturalization should be considered as one piece of the jigsaw that is closing off the United States to nonwhite individuals. Beginning with the Muslim ban, now upheld by the Supreme Court, extending to the vastly sped up ICE raids in areas with large Latino populations, to the detention and separation of asylum-seeking families at the border, these bits and pieces come together to reveal a worldview that accords with white nationalism.[7]

Zakaria notes that two operations have emerged for this purpose. The first is the Janus Operation, based in Los Angeles; as of this writing this operation has created over twenty-five hundred cases that have been reported for prosecution and that may result in denaturalization. The second is Operation Second Look, which, as Zakaria notes, "will review hundreds of thousands of petitions to locate the tiniest of discrepancies" in order to denaturalize U.S. citizens.

The U.S. Immigration and Customs Enforcement, or ICE, which is the police arm of both Janus and Operation Second Look, has attempted to keep its officers' field manual away from the public, and with good reason. The handbook could be used in court to show how ICE's push to lead on denaturalization cases stands in contrast to the language of federal law governing the process, not to mention Fourteenth Amendment protections that demand due process under the law. Yet the Trump administration is proceeding despite the Supreme Court's judgment in the 1964 *Schneider v. Rusk* case that it is "impermissible" to assume "that naturalized citizens as a class are less reliable and bear less allegiance to this country than do the native born."[8] One of the most publicized cases involves Trump's crackdown on "midwife-issued birth certificates." While midwife-facilitated births in the Southwest are common as a result of historical tradition, as well as lack of medical care along the U.S.-Mexico border, the Trump administration is putting these specific births in question as never before. While concerns about spurious birth certificates weren't created by the Trump administration, journalist Dara Lind notes that under Trump there is a new "surge" in denying passports to people who have U.S. birth certificates and have lived in the United States all their lives.[9] The ICE denaturalization handbook, recently obtained by activists and scholars through a Freedom of Information Act (FOIA) request, "makes clear that the priority for ICE's investigative division, Homeland Security Investigations ... in denaturalization proceedings is to use the most efficient means possible to fulfill a single-minded goal: leveraging the bureau-cratic process to strip citizenship from naturalized Americans."[10] While this ICE directive is stunning in and of itself, it is equally stunning that it has remained largely unremarked in the media. Not surprisingly, Latinos are largely bearing the brunt of this latest denaturalization assault against U.S. citizens, Supreme Court precedent notwithstanding.

In the history of the United States, denaturalization has been rare and reserved only for the most serious cases, such as those of war criminals or former Nazis. Trumpism has ushered in an age when the president himself can call white nationalists and neo-Nazis "fine people," but Brown people are always already suspect, and this should alert us to the seriousness of the crisis at hand, in which ignoring historical cause-effect relations has deadly consequences for citizens, citizens in the making, and the futures of the democratic commons. But how could this come to pass? How is it possible that structures and institutions such as our educational system and our laws, entrusted to fortify and protect the democratic commons, are seemingly working against the foundational hallmarks of democratic practice?

THE RICHWINE CONTROVERSY

It might seem that anti-Latino racism was enshrined when Univision reporter Jorge Ramos was "deported" by Trump at a press briefing after Ramos asked him why he had called Mexicans and Latinos "rapists and murderers." But its scaffolding can be traced to neocon think tanks and the work of their "scholar-fellows" (see author website, figure 1). The focus has been consistent since the late 1970s and organized around the following: limiting immigration; establishing the "inferiority" of minorities through contemporary "research" on IQ, race, and eugenics; eliminating affirmative action; building conservative student coalitions against "multiculturalism" on campuses; and tort reform that favors deregulation.[11] In their classic study documenting this social-engineering phenomenon created by the antidemocratic radical right, Jean Stefancic and Richard Delgado were eerily prescient: "Women's gains will be rolled back, foreigners will be excluded ... conservative judges, appointed by conservative presidents with the encouragement of a conservative Congress, will repeal prisoners' and children's rights, and narrow women's procreative liberties."[12] Stefancic and Delgado's early warnings have arrived at our doorstep, and we are seemingly ill prepared to the meet the demands at hand. Latinos are certainly not the only target of these assaults, but Latinos are the most vulnerable insofar there is no sustained public sphere discussion or defined policy agenda to tackle these challenges. Let me illustrate the conundrum through an emblematic example.

Political commentator Jason Richwine has responded to the exigencies of the Latino question by laying the groundwork for the current racist assault and divestment of Latinos through alt-right pseudoscience. He has done so in ways that eerily parallel early eugenicist "research," setting the stage for the emergence of the full-on racism evidenced during and after Trump's election. Richwine's "scholarship" perpetuated the erroneous assumption that all Latinos are recent arrivals—and likely "illegal" immigrants—in a coauthored Heritage Foundation report that put a $6.3 trillion price tag on a proposed 2013 Senate immigration reform proposal. Since then the report has taken on a life of its own. (It served as the basis for the "alternative realities" that eventually allowed Trump to find the support for his "Mexican wall"—before and after the election—by promising that he would prevent Mexican "rapists and murderers" from entering the country.) The report came under scrutiny not only for its grossly exaggerated partisan claims, but also because it was discovered that Richwine had previously written a Harvard University dissertation that claimed that Latino immigrants did not possess the intelligence quotient to make them assimilable into the American body politic, despite the nation's great efforts to assimilate them. In that dissertation, Richwine claimed that

> low IQ and socioeconomic status has *[sic]* persisted among Hispanics through several generations since 1965, with few signs of improvement. This invites comparison to early twentieth century immigrants from Europe, who were also thought by some to have inferior intelligence levels compared to natives. Today the descendants of those European immigrants are highly similar to the "founding stock" on most measures. The optimistic view of post-1965 immigration is that Hispanic IQ will rise as environments improve, and assimilation will take place much as it did for those Europeans who came a century ago. Unfortunately, that view is misguided.[13]

In his dissertation, Richwine asserted that Latinos, along with Blacks, are simply intellectually inferior to whites and have trouble assimilating because of a supposed genetic predisposition to lower IQ scores, making them incapable of meeting the basic standards of the nation's "founding stock." Clearly for Richwine, "Hispanic immigrants" are interchangeable with all Latinos, immigrants or not, despite the continuous presence of peoples of Latin American ancestry in this country from its founding to our present; moreover, he relegates the country's indigenous first nations (the nation's original "founding stock") to historical oblivion or, at best, irrelevance.[14] In his dissertation at Harvard University's Kennedy School of Government, Richwine deployed "race" as a term whose meaning is stable over time, not as a historically contingent category whose meanings change depending on historical context, as if somehow race, or racial difference, had the same contemporary meaning for members of the KKK as it did for members of the NAACP in, say, the 1960s or even today. Equally disturbing is his unsubstantiated assertion that there has been little improvement in the IQ scores of Hispanics since 1965. The signal year of 1965 should have been significant, not inconsequential, to Richwine's study insofar as it marked the signing of the Voting Rights Act, which, along with the Civil Rights Act of 1964, was to herald President Johnson's Great Society: a nation free of poverty and systemic racial injustice.[15] Ignoring this tremendous national victory for the instantiation and potential of democratic freedom and equality—if not altogether negating both the Civil Rights Act and the Voting Right Act's arduous processes of implementation or the historical accounting initiated by Johnson's call for a Great Society—Richwine safely survived a dissertation defense that ignored decades of social science research by contending that both IQ and "race" are stable, "scientific" categories. As Michael P. Jefferies has reminded us in *Paint the White House Black* (2013), "No matter the time and place, race is intimately bound with the distribution of rights and resources, and racial ideas are manifest in social inequalities," a fact lost on Richwine's impressive display of historical and scientific ignorance in a dissertation at one of the nation's most important and venerated research universities.[16] The seal of approval as a Harvard-educated "researcher" was significant because it brought Richwine into the fold of prominent neocon circles and led to the outspoken support for his work by Charles Murray, the modern-day eugenicist and "research fellow" of the American Enterprise Institute, a neocon think tank.

After defending his dissertation, Richwine continued his investment in the divestiture of Latinos—writ large—from

American public life. Shortly after the announcement of Sotomayor's nomination in 2009, he took it upon himself to remind his readers at the *American,* the American Enterprise Institute's online publication, that conservatives should not be chastised for asserting that the likes of Supreme Court nominee Sonia Sotomayor is "an intellectual lightweight who [lacks] the brainpower to be an effective justice," since questioning the IQ of opponents is a tactic and "a specialty of liberals."[17] Though Richwine's invective against liberals—and of Sotomayor as a potentially inadequate "Hispanic" nominee to the Supreme Court—steered clear of directly assessing Sotomayor's intellect, its presence and his broader work reflected that Latinos can be bashed with impunity. The Heritage Foundation ultimately distanced itself from Richwine's dissertation, saying it did not reflect its positions, and Richwine ultimately resigned, but not before he went on to consult for President Trump to provide the "scientific" basis for Latino "inferiority" and the concomitant literal violence enacted against Black and Brown bodies.[18]

Throughout the controversy, and well after his resignation, Richwine doggedly maintained that he was not a racist and that he stood by his "research findings." Not surprisingly, his early supporter and mentor, Charles Murray, also came to his defense. Murray called Richwine's forced resignation from the Heritage Foundation an example of "a corruption that [had] spread throughout American intellectual discourse" that made it nearly impossible to state "scientific proof" in the face of antiscientific "political correctness." Murray, with Richard Hernstein, infamously wrote *The Bell Curve: Intelligence and Class Structure in American Life* (1994)—a book that claimed that Blacks have lower levels of intelligence than the rest of the population. He went on to defend his mentee, saying that the dissertation that secured

Richwine's appointment as a Heritage Foundation fellow "had meticulously assembled and analyzed the test-score data, which showed exactly what [Richwine] said they showed: mean IQ-score differences between Latinos and non-Latino whites" demonstrated Latino intellectual inferiority.[19] While Murray does not consider himself or Richwine "racists" but merely messengers of "science," what emerges in such considerations of purported Latino or Black intellectual inferiority is that historically factual racism cannot be used to inveigh against "scientific" pronouncements of biological determinism (i.e., the belief that Latinos and Blacks are "stupid"). For the likes of Murray and Richwine, it is possible to consider themselves "nonracists," and their work "scientific," even as they presumably pity Latinos and Blacks for their intellectual inferiority, though perhaps not more than they pity themselves for being the victims of "political correctness" and "reverse discrimination." That the "research" undertaken by the Richwines and Murrays of today could be put to racist ends, as in Richwine's Heritage Foundation report, seems of no consequence to these stalwarts of scientific reason because their version of scientific proof cannot be burdened with the consequences of diminishing those they deem inferior or, even less, with understanding how rampant inequality diminishes all Americans. Neither Richwine nor Murray seems to think it is politically consequential to ascribe disadvantages to qualities they believe to be intrinsic to Latinos and Blacks, even if such a thing could be proved. And they do not consider how those disadvantages are mediated by social interactions governed by years of discrimination sanctioned in and through laws, because for them the roots of inequality reside in these groups' unequal intelligence. What would the United States of America be if the "intellectually feeble," as described by Richwine and

Murray, exercised their rights to full citizenship, or simply sought the full practice of citizenship? The Richwines and the Murrays have an answer that would make both Latinos and Blacks dead political subjects, irrespective of their citizenship status, and make them beholden to the nation's white "founding stock," as understood by the contemporary racist regime.

As the self-appointed arbiters of a new Ellis Island seeped in contemporary eugenics as the means through which to delimit full personhood in the democratic commons, Murray and Richwine continue a longer racialized history of attempting to discern the real or putative cognitive (dis)abilities of immigrants or Black nationals whom they cast as always already dead citizens who burden the state. It appears that it is infinitely more beneficial today to not *be* a racist but to merely consider arenas as diverse as economic and educational policy, infant mortality, and access to health care not as racialized and exclusionary domestic norms but as being within equal reach of all people, provided they have the intelligence to reap the democratically dispensed plenty before them. For Richwine and Murray, any evidence of diminished opportunities and life chances parsed along ethnoracial lines can simply be chalked up to the vagaries of "innate intelligence." Indeed, the opportunity hoarding that such engagements with "science" enact is not just about reinstating the privilege of what they believe to be the nation's so-called founding stock (read: Anglo-Americans). Rather, it is rooted in the violent and concomitant historical amnesias that continue to subtend our country's whitewashing, which both paralyzes our current political discourse and forecloses the possibility of ethical democratic practice for the greater good. It is simply of no consequence to them that peer-reviewed research has directly correlated academic success and top scores in predictors of

"intelligence," such as the SAT and ACT, to the zip codes associated with well-resourced schools.[20]

Regardless of the sincerity of their stated belief that they are
not racists—they routinely acknowledge that certain individuals
can diverge from the "predispositions" of their group affiliation—
both Richwine and Murray assert the potential for Latinos and
Blacks to counter the very stereotypes these authors have perpetuated and repackaged for us in the twenty-first century. In so
doing they establish the pretext for recognizing the exception that
proves the rule. Obama and Sotomayor function as just such
exceptions for our moment in this narrative of "bootstraps" and
racial biological determinism that is ostensibly not racist because
it is purportedly "scientific." Despite the public embarrassment
surrounding the Richwine controversy, the corporatist Heritage
Foundation held fast to its immigration report, according to which
any amnesty for undocumented workers would likely bankrupt
the nation and privilege "unlawful immigrants" over "true"
Americans.[21] Not surprisingly, the report continues to be a fixture
among the more "scholarly" alt-right neocons of the moment who
see building a wall along the U.S.-Mexico border as a profitable
venture, not unlike building more prisons. If this seems like an
overstatement, let us refer to the evidence at hand while we still
can. The prototype of the Trump wall is being built by an Israeli
company, ELTA North America, the same company that builds
walls along the Gaza Strip and whose subsidiaries serve as the
largest contractor for building the United States' prison industrial
complex (see author website, figure 2).[22]

In the reigning moment of state-sanctioned racism, what soci-
ologist Eduardo Bonilla-Silva calls "racism without racists," the
Heritage Foundation report that Richwine coauthored could be
said to simply be stating the facts if viewed a certain way, or offer-

ing "alternative facts," as Kellyanne Conway, counselor to the president, called it early on in the Trump administration's disavowal of reality.[23] Viewed another way, however, racism is not about personal "feelings" but about verifiable cause-effect relations and quantifiable resultant facts; we would thus say that the country's most disenfranchised minorities are and have almost always been structurally excluded from the purported plenty before them. As Bonilla-Silva has asserted, this new racism without racists

> has become a formidable political tool for the maintenance of the racial order. Much as Jim Crow racism served as the glue for defending a brutal and overt system of racial oppression in the pre-Civil Rights era, color-blind racism serves today as the ideological armor for a covert and institutionalized system in the post–Civil Rights era. And the beauty of this new ideology is that it aids in the maintenance of white privilege without fanfare, without naming those who it subjects and those who it rewards.[24]

For the Murrays, Richwines, and racists of our moment, the ideals of the civil rights movement are *the* problem, since that movement sought to ameliorate if not altogether end institutionalized inequality. Also problematic for them is the importance of impartial research for the public good. And their "ideological" positions are regrettably representative of a broader cultural turn in which ideology creates "facts," not the other way around.

Though I have focused on the Richwine controversy in this chapter for its ability to encapsulate the state of the Latino question before and after Trump's election, I could have just as easily chosen dozens of other telling and recent attempts at addressing the Latino question in a variety of public media by liberals and conservatives alike.[25] The Richwine response to the Latino question and its institutionalization is nonetheless fundamentally instructive insofar as it speaks to what passes in public discourse as "respectable" and "thoughtful" commentary in our historical moment, as opposed to the less than informed assertions that we have come to associate with untempered internet drivel, and the more obviously partisan media outlets of our day that traffic in "deepfake" news. Indeed, unlike African American public intellectuals who have the media and the moral scaffolding to counter such attacks, Latino intellectuals lack a viable presence in the public sphere, which is why the stories of inclusion offered by exemplary Latinos such as Sotomayor are so compelling. This is so not just because Sotomayor's narrative represents an exceptional American story of accomplishment despite insurmountable odds, but precisely because there are so few Latinos who can counter the heavy weight of institutional disenfranchisement from the fiber of American public life, who can put the lie to the proscriptive racism of Richwine and his ilk.

Given the state of the Latino question, what tools can we employ so as not to despair in the face of such pessimism brought about by the unrelenting assault on the Latino body politic? Beyond the purposeful commitment to democratic practice and ethical historical accounting, and beyond aspirational representative figures, we would do well to recenter a largely forgotten but signal Supreme Court case known as *Hernández v. Texas.*

BEING BROWN IN 1954: *BROWN V. BOARD OF EDUCATION* AND *HERNÁNDEZ V. TEXAS*

Sonia Sotomayor was born in a signal year in U.S. civil rights history. First, the landmark 1954 Supreme Court case *Brown v. Board of Education* enshrined one of the cornerstones of the civil rights movement by establishing that "separate but equal" education was not equal at all but discriminatory and requiring legal remedy. The *Brown v. Board of Education* case allowed the first Black Supreme Court associate justice, Thurgood Marshall (1908–1993), to expand on "stare decisis," that is, established legal precedent, to shepherd the case by referring to another case that preceded Brown by eight years, *Mendez v. Westminster* (1946). Briefly, the *Mendez v. Westminster* decision involved a Mexican American child, Sylvia Mendez, who was turned away from a California public school for "whites only." Her father, Gonzalo Mendez, took four Los Angeles school districts to court and won a class action suit. The case was significant for several reasons. The Mendez family attorney, David C. Marcus, took the unprecedented step at the time of presenting social science evidence in support of his argument. His evidence proved in the trial, and later on appeal, that segregation resulted in "feelings" of inferiority among Mexican American children that could undermine their ability to be productive American citizens. The presiding U.S. District Court judge, Paul J. McCormick, agreed and ordered that the school districts cease their "discriminatory practices against the pupils of Mexican descent in the public schools."[26] The Mendez case proved, however anachronistically, and to invoke José Esteban Muñoz's work again, that "being Brown" was a condition of being in the world that had contextual anchors in practices that contained Brown bodies and consequently required legal remediation in order to allow Sylvia Mendez access to the possibility of "feeling" as though she could have a productive civic life (understood as productive "American" citizenship).

Building on previous Supreme Court decisions that established equal protection under the law, the *Hernández v. Texas* case was world making for Brown bodies, since it extended Fourteenth

Amendment protections to people of Latin American ancestry in the United States. The case shows the degree to which legal discourse can gesture toward reparative forms of justice. As Joshua Chambers-Letson has noted in his important analysis of Sotomayor's entry into civic life, "U.S. law has played a significant role in shaping what types of bodies represent the nation, and by extension, should represent the rule of law in the high court."[27] Not insignificantly, Sotomayor, despite her story of meritocratic success, was appointed by a Black president whose own legitimacy was questioned by the radical right and fringe "birthers" who claimed Obama wasn't a "real American," which allowed conspiracy theories to direct public discourse about birthright citizenship in the service of craven ends through expediency, rather than in the greater service of the democratic commons. It is for this reason that we cannot underestimate how the *Hernández v. Texas* case reached the stunning conclusion that it did in 1954. To understand its importance, it will be necessary to contextualize its significance.

Pedro "Pete" Hernández was an agricultural worker who was indicted for the murder of José "Joe" Espinoza by an all-white jury in Jackson County, Texas. In the initial trial, Hernández's attorneys, Carlos C. Cadena and Gustavo "Gus" Garcia, built a case by establishing a common-practice fact: that Mexican Americans were barred from the jury commission that selected juries, and that, consequently, Hernández was denied a jury of his peers. Cadena and Garcia sought to establish that a Mexican American had not served on a jury in Jackson County in over twenty-five years, thereby hoping to establish that citizens of Mexican ancestry were discriminated against as a special class. Cadena took the lead in drafting the Hernández appeal. His tightly argued legal brief elaborated a novel theory that

Mexican Americans, though white, were "a class apart." Cadena wrote in the appeal that the only times that Mexicans, "many of them Texans for seven generations, are covered with the Caucasian cloak, is when it serves the ends of those who would shamelessly deny this large segment of the Texas population their fundamental rights."[28] The trial court, however, denied the motions, and Hernández was found guilty of murder and sentenced by the all-white jury to life in prison. In affirming the lower court's ruling, the Texas Court of Criminal Appeals found that "Mexicans are ... members of and within the classification of the white race as distinguished from members of the Negro Race," thereby rejecting Cadena and Garcia's argument that Mexican Americans were a "special class" under the meaning of the Fourteenth Amendment.

The case eventually reached the Supreme Court. In Michael A. Olivas's important book about the Hernández case, he writes,

> On January 11, 1954, Gus Garcia and Carlos Cadena argued Hernandez; in what was unprecedented at the time, Garcia was given 12 minutes more than was usually allowed for oral arguments. According to observers, he was brilliant in his oratory. Two weeks later Brown was argued before the same Court by Thurgood Marshall, with a much larger audience and international attention.[29]

In a unanimous opinion delivered by Chief Justice Earl Warren (1891–1974), the Supreme Court held that the Fourteenth Amendment protects those beyond the two classes of "white or Negro," thereby extending Fourteenth Amendment protections to peoples of Latin American ancestry or other racial groups, if it could be proved that "special class" discrimination exists: "When the existence of a distinct class is demonstrated, and it is further shown that the laws, as written or as applied, single out that class

for different treatment not based on some reasonable classification, the guarantees of the Constitution have been violated."
Astoundingly, the Supreme Court established that the Constitution's Fourteenth Amendment is not directed solely against discrimination due to a "two-class theory"—the Black and white of
it, as it were—but that it covers those of Mexican and Latin
American ancestry. This is significant because the Fourteenth
Amendment is the primary legal battlefield on which judicial
restraint and judicial action have come to blows. The legal principle of stare decisis *(stare et non quieta movere)*, meaning "to stand by
decisions and not disturb the undisturbed," proved to be two-
sided in this unusual case. Standing by precedent would simply be
an injustice. Historically speaking, the case demonstrates that the
Supreme Court's "judicial action" was necessary because Mexican Americans and, by extension, what today we call "Latinos"
were a special "class apart." In so doing, the court recognized that
historical evidence undermined the veneer of legal impartiality.
Quite simply, Latinos had not been treated impartially by the law.
The implications of the *Hernández v. Texas* decision were and continue to be world making for both the history and the futures of
the Brown commons. For the first time in the country's history,
Latinos—again, people of Latin American ancestry in the United
States—were afforded the same protections as had African Americans after the U.S. Civil War (1861–65). The antecedents of the
case are equally striking.

Hernández v. Texas was supported by the League of United
Latin American Citizens (LULAC), and the connection merits
commentary. LULAC was founded in 1929 to support Mexican
Americans. Given the structural racism inherent to "being" Mexican or Mexican American at the time of the organization's founding, the name of the organization emphasized "Latin America," as

opposed to Mexico or *Mexicanness,* in order to distance LULAC from the public sphere's conception of Mexicans as "Blacks who speak a different language." This strategic conceit is deeply problematic but historically meaningful if understood as a type of strategic essentialism. The lawyers for the case had a strategy as risky as it was innovative. Arguing for the constitutional protection of "Mexican Americans" meant that they would need to affirm that Mexican Americans were treated as less than white even though they were ostensibly "white" under the law. In other words, the strategy required that they paradoxically emphasize their structural proximity to whiteness while at the same time emphasizing the degrees of whiteness within the judicial justice system that rendered Mexican Americans "less than" white, somewhere between Black and white; let us call it *Brown* territory. In so doing, they put their very social and historical identity on trial by hingeing their case on a *brownness* that was not yet legible within the criminal justice system. This is significant insofar as LULAC's strategy paid off by establishing the basis for an "off-white ethnic identity" recognized by the court as the root of disparate treatment under the law, one deserving of Fourteenth Amendment protections.

We should note that after the U.S.-Mexico War (1846–48), Mexico lost almost half of its territories to the United States. After U.S. conquest and empire building, Mexicans in the newly consolidated territories of the United States began to elaborate a complex relationship to Anglo-American domination. The annexed Mexican territories included present-day California, Utah, Nevada, and Texas, as well as parts of Arizona, Colorado, New Mexico, and Wyoming. This inaugural moment in U.S. empire building created crisis moments and related survival strategies as the possibilities for entry into civic life and national belonging began to be organized around an axis of race, as opposed to the category of citizenship in jurisprudence. It is for this reason, for example, that the national signifier "Mexican" became a racial designation in the United States rather than one of national affiliation as the question of "slave" versus "free" states both dominated and delimited democratic participation along the Black-white binary we have inherited from the Civil War to our Trumpian present. In the process, what today we would understand as the "Latino body" became an exchangeable commodity under capital as Mexicans, and peoples of Latin American ancestry in the United States, began to be classed as "Blacks."[30] While it would be impolitic for LULAC to acknowledge the history it ran from, it behooves us to understand why its own delimiting fictions enabled the instantiation of the only Supreme Court case to unequivocally render Latino life both protected and legible with the broader American body politic. That the *Hernández v. Texas* case was decided months before Operation Wetback, the largest recorded deportation in American history, should remind us of the limits of national incorporation.[31] Operation Wetback, from the start of the deportations in the summer of 1954 and before the close of the year, resulted in the removal of over one million Mexicans, Mexican Americans citizens, resident aliens, and guest workers. The arc of the moral universe bends toward justice, but we should be prepared to confront the forces that attempt to halt its progression with ethical precision and historical clarity.

It is a curious historical fact that Latino advocacy groups and universalists have largely ignored the legacies of *Hernández v. Texas.* We may continue to ignore this significant antecedent for its paradoxically messy disavowals of *Mexicanness* and *blackness,* but we would do so at our own peril. To paraphrase Michel Foucault's assertion from *The History of Sexuality,* volume 1, there is no "outside of power" and, as such, no pure subject positions from which to counter power without engaging the logics of power. *Hernández v. Texas* constitutes both a tool and a point of entry for historicizing and protecting basic Latino civil rights that we would have otherwise assumed only some years ago to be simply a given: that Latino life matters. The current national crisis in meaning about the dignity of all Americans, especially the most vulnerable, requires that we respond with ethical clarity, measured intelligence, and absolute resolve.

It is tempting to understand Sotomayor's life story as a sweeping democratic embrace that would allow us to imagine a country capable of delivering on the American dream to its aspirants— along with the belief in the imperative of democratic equality of access that fuels our national narratives of progress—in a historical moment of profound demographic and political transformations and, as I have shown, unimaginable racism and disdain for and against Latinos. For both Latinos and the country, the stakes are high. Latinos and other citizens, or cultural citizens in the making, may be moved and inspired by Sotomayor's "bootstrap" narratives, especially given the dispossession of Latinos from American life. The comfort that such a compelling narrative provides, however, would be short lived once the evidence at hand comes into focus. For this reason it is necessary to explore why this minoritarian story may very well make us apathetic to the messy work of *being Brown*, which is about being "woke" in the democratic commons. Such an awakening is the only ethical response in the face of the violence before us. As we have learned from the courage of our African American counterparts, claiming a space within the democratic commons is a matter of life and death. But you must not despair. Such an understanding of our connectedness to a history of loss and subjection, our own and that of others, should not bind us to history as a foregone conclusion. On the contrary, it must move us to turn that history to different purposes. We must therefore endeavor to account for how this history came to be, and what we stand to lose if we allow symbolic inclusion to supplant the exacting demands that lived political enfranchisement requires of us all. Such are the responsibilities that the Latino question demands of us.

CHAPTER TWO

Sonia Sotomayor's Elusive Embrace

The higher education crisis in the United States
points to the demise of opportunity and the
emergence of a society with caste-like characteristics.

Suzanne Mettler[1]

Sonia Sotomayor's exceptional life story of resolve and accomplishment in the face of seemingly insurmountable odds has made her an imitable American. Her ascent from the Bronx tenement where she was raised as the child of Puerto Rican migrants to the pinnacle of national institutions as a U.S. Supreme Court associate justice—being only the third woman to be appointed to the court—has already had an impact on how the national culture understands its relationship to Latino communities. Indeed, Sotomayor's rise from poverty through education, dogged determination, hard work, and the adoption of a Puritan work ethnic has resonated with national constituencies on both the left and right of the political divide. No less significantly, it has also resonated with disenfranchised national communities who rarely see themselves positively reflected in the mirror of American cultural history.

The heft and reach of Sotomayor's poignant life story as a representative Latina is particularly significant if we consider what the nation and Latinos stand to gain by at last having a long-delayed national discussion about the Latino question. Such a discussion might allow us to understand why Latinos— again, at over 57.5 million strong—are still the most underrepresented group in American institutions and are en bloc the least likely to graduate from high school, not to mention college.[2] Given the invisibility of Latinos in American civic life, along with the mass appeal of Sotomayor's life story to diverse national constituencies of all political stripes, it should come as no surprise that she has become a national sensation with a story of uplift that has resonated deeply in a political moment steeped in economic crisis, frayed civic bonds, and increasingly heightened ethnic and racial tensions. Sotomayor's exemplary life narrative allows all Americans to imagine a country in which we all belong as constitutive subjects of the American body politic. Quite simply, Sotomayor's life story heartily encapsulates the American dream of social mobility and the promise of democratic inclusion.[3] And it is the principal story she lovingly tells in her stunningly successful memoir, *My Beloved World* (2013).

After its publication in January 2013, *My Beloved World* quickly became a *New York Times* nonfiction best seller, and its author, a seemingly natural book-circuit doyenne.[4] Traveling from coast to coast on her book tour, Sotomayor defied the image of the cloistered and detached Supreme Court justice to become the "people's justice." In the process, she developed a reputation as one of the most accessible justices in the country's history. Commenting on her extensive book tour, a reporter went so far as to call Sotomayor the "queen of the best-seller list" and, not inconsequentially, "the nation's most high-profile Hispanic figure."[5]

Her memoir further solidified her standing as the most recognizable Latino figure in the country in addition to the considerable popularity she had already garnered as the subject of motivational and popular biographies. She also appeared as a guest on shows as diverse as *The View, 60 Minutes,* and *Sesame Street,* and she became the inspiration for books such as *Wise Latina: Writers on Higher Education* (2014), edited by Jennifer De Leon, not to mention poetry, jazz orchestra songs, and even a biographical graphic novel created by Puerto Rican artist César Feliciano for the popular "Amazing Women" series. Sotomayor herself considers that, although she hopes to "write opinions that will last the ages," her most important contribution will be "the impact on people who feel inspired in any way by me."[6] Sotomayor's commitment to inspiring the various communities she seeks to reach has also made her a de facto motivational speaker for scores of Latinos starved for images of success beyond sports and entertainment who are doggedly determined to believe that progress and economic mobility are possible as long as you believe in the possibilities underwritten by the American dream. And her book tours and related speaking engagements have allowed her to do just that: to inspire people to believe in her message of hope, sometimes moving people to tears, as anyone who has attended her public talks can attest.

In the various versions of Sotomayor's life story of advancement through educational achievement—from the graphic novel to her moving memoir to the various versions in between—the American dream has served as the principal framing device. Sotomayor's invocation of the American dream also functions as both a performance of and an attachment to a particular American patriotic identity premised on assimilation. Sotomayor's invocation, it must be plainly stated from the onset, adheres to an epistemology grounded in a national and political paradigm of economic advancement that presumes equality of access to all nationals who aspire to the dream's promises irrespective of their gender orientation, linguistic particularisms, or sexual, ethnic, or racial identity. The strength of the American dream's various invocations in the stories surrounding Sotomayor's tremendous achievements has made her one of the most emblematic recent historical figures through whom the character and promise of American social and political inclusion can be recast anew for citizens, as well as for the scores of undocumented aspirants to citizenship who have been consistently excluded from the promise of an all too exhausted dream of inclusion and mobility. Since Sotomayor's story of success through educational achievement is so steeped in the mythology of boundless possibilities that the American dream ostensibly affords, it becomes necessary to understand both the promise and the limits that the dream holds for the various communities her story so poignantly speaks to.

AMERICAN DREAMS OF SOCIAL MOBILITY

The American dream is one of the foundational markers of our national identity and has served as one of the most compelling and unifying narratives to emerge from the nation's founding moment. Alexis de Tocqueville (1805–59) referred to it as "the lure of anticipated success" in his foundational study of American institutions, *Democracy in America* (1840). Tocqueville was, of course, delineating the progression of a national ideal that had been codified and enshrined in the country's cultural memory from the Declaration of Independence to his writing moment. It is an ideal that has survived in the public imagination as a series of aphorisms about our national identity: "all men are created equal" and have the "unalienable right" to the "pursuit of happiness." These founding conceits are part of a national mythology that has been transmitted generation after generation by presidents, pundits, and teachers to schoolchildren and scores of citizens, and citizens in the making, who come from every imaginable socioeconomic rank. The American dream and the words the dream indexes tell a story about what it means to both *be* an American and *how* to believe in America as an idea. If you come to America, the myth holds, and you work hard and play by the rules, you can build a good life. The dream functions as the unwritten promise that all residents of the United States have a reasonable chance of achieving success though their own efforts, talents, and hard work. In America, so the story goes, it is still possible for anyone to achieve their dreams of success provided they have the ambition and determination to make their ambitions a reality. Those who do not, however, are considered victims of their own sloth, lack of talent, or bad luck, but not the victims of institutional initiatives, laws, mandates, or the resultant social stigmas occasioned by histories of national racial or ethnic prejudice.

Though the reiterative quality of the American dream narrative is most often defined in terms of material and economic success, it is infinitely adaptable to what anyone can imagine for him- or herself. It is a powerful narrative that is inculcated from our earliest educational experiences and posits the centrality of education and individual drive as the principal vehicles through which to achieve the dream's promise. Because the American dream is such a powerful story in its promise of the boundless possibilities for self-making and achievement, it has also been traditionally one of the most resistant to scrutiny, despite considerable academic critique and scholarship on the topic. Our current economic crisis and the concomitant shrinking of the middle class have, however, made that dream more elusive and difficult to believe in than ever before. Hedrick Smith has gone so far as to suggest that the "soaring wealth of the super rich has brought the unraveling of the American dream for the middle class" and created a stratified, caste-like system. This is so because education, once the principal vehicle for the American dream's survival, no longer serves as either the path of entry into the middle class or the predictor of economic stability.[7] In his influential and less than ambiguously titled *Who Stole the American Dream?* (2012), Smith contends that "one major reason that a caste society is emerging in the United States is that education is no longer the great social leveler that it once was."[8] Education, "the great social leveler," as Smith calls it, is no longer the American dream's vehicle for economic and social success. If education was the great social and economic leveler that allowed the American dream to thrive as Smith contends, then we would do well to understand why it has failed such a large swath of the population and, in particular, why it has failed the nation's most disenfranchised minority majority.

Educational studies researcher Jennifer Hochschild has calibrated both the meaning and the limits of the American dream and its indebtedness to educational access. In her classic study, *The American Dream and the Public Schools* (2003), Hochschild reads our national mythology as a political ideology premised on three unexamined suppositions: that the opportunity for social and economic mobility is equal for each individual; that the United States is a meritocratic society; and that both success and failure are individually determined and deserved. Hochschild contends that the American dream is a brilliant ideological invention, although ... in practice it leaves much to be desired. Its power depends partly on the way it balances individual and collective responsibilities. The role of the government is to make the pursuit of success possible for everyone. This implies strict and complete nondiscrimination, universal education to provide the means for pursuing success, and protection for virtually all views of success, regardless of how many people endorse them. The state also has to create and preserve democratic institutions, including schools.... The polity, in short, has to create the conditions that make the dream appealing, possible, and viable for future generations.[9]

The conditions of possibility for making that dream plausible, not to mention viable, are in short supply, as Hochschild understands it. That reality notwithstanding, the conditions that for Hochschild subtend the American dream continue to have a profound effect on our national expectations and what we believe about those who cannot reach the dream's promise or even aspire to it. I am interested in invoking Hochschild's critique of populist renderings of the American dream for two principal reasons. First, her work encapsulates the considerable literature about the promise and limits of the American dream and relates them to the fundamental tenets of social and civic mobility through education, tenets that are central to Sotomayor's iteration of her own version of the dream of social and economic success. Second, Hochschild's analysis is particularly significant because the dream of education as the great social leveler has historically been far more elusive for Latinos than for any other group. Let me explain why.

In our current historical moment the dream of civic and economic inclusion for Latinos has become politically charged and rife with intense partisan and racial polarization, volatile political battles, and rising xenophobic diatribes against Latino citizens as well as those Latino cultural citizens who are either legal residents or undocumented social actors. Yet even though Latinos are the nation's largest minority, and are no longer the "sleeping giant" of electoral politics, as they were characterized in the national political landscape before President Obama's reelection in 2012, "Americans" continue to view Latinos as recent intruders into the national fold. Indeed, for most Americans the term *Latino*, or its more imprecise analogue *Hispanic* in common parlance, is simply synonymous with *illegal immigrant*. As recent polling shows, one out of three Americans inaccurately believes that *all* Latinos are undocumented, though over 64 percent of all Latinos are native-born U.S. citizens.[10] How can this be? That Latinos have been in this geopolitical territory called the United States since before the arrival of the Puritans makes our present historical amnesia both shamefully telling, and it prevents us from apprehending how and why we have deprived ourselves of a significant part of our cultural history, our inescapable present, and our inevitable future.[11]

Given the current state of historical misapprehension and ignorance about Latinos, it is easy to see why Sotomayor's life story is rendered exceptional, especially regarding what she has accomplished and how she inspires many as a representative Latina, a woman of color, and an exemplary American. Yet the historical context also makes her exceptionally noteworthy for another set of reasons that have been conspicuously absent from the uncritical exuberance that has surrounded her spectacular story of educational achievement and success. According to the National Center for Education Statistics, Latinos fail to graduate from high school more than any other ethnic or racial group, even though the U.S. graduation rate is at an all-time high. And of those Latinos who do graduate from high school, only about

18 percent enroll in college—an enrollment rate lower than that of any other ethnic or racial group.[12] The graduation rate of Latino college students is equally disturbing. In 2010, for example, when Sotomayor completed her first year on the Supreme Court, the graduation rate for Latino college students ages 25 to 29 was 13.5 percent, compared with 38.6 percent for whites, 19.4 percent for African Americans, and 52.5 percent for Asian Americans.[13] This is significant because there is a staggering wage gap between workers with only a high school education and those who are college educated. After Sotomayor graduated from Yale in 1979, for example, the average worker with a college degree "earned 38% more than the average high school graduate. By 2000, the college high school graduate wage gap increased to 57%, and by 2011 it rose to 73%."[14]

Quite simply, the conditions under which Sotomayor could flourish as a beneficiary of affirmative action and reap the benefits of the American dream do not exist for the great majority of Latino citizens, cultural citizens, or aspirants to citizenship. What remains of "affirmative action," as a social and educational policy to enfranchise those who have borne the brunt of historical discrimination, has simply been deracinated. Understanding how this came to be helps frame both the promise and the limits of Sotomayor's educational trajectory and the broader story of Latino access to education and social mobility.

SOTOMAYOR AND THE LEGACIES OF AFFIRMATIVE ACTION

When the anger, the upset, and the agitation had passed, a certainty remained: I had no need to apologize that the look-wider, search-more affirmative action that Princeton and Yale practiced had opened

> doors for me.... I had been admitted to the Ivy
> League through a special door, and I had more
> ground than most to make up before I was with my
> classmates on an equal footing.
> Sonia Sotomayor[15]

Sotomayor is clear about the benefits of "affirmative action" in her own story of educational achievement and civic enfranchisement. The implementation of affirmative action in American higher education, that "special door," as Sotomayor calls it in her memoir, gave her educational opportunities that would not have been available to her if institutions—especially those as privileged as Princeton and Yale—had not instituted affirmative action policies.[16] At its core, affirmative action sought to increase the representation of women and minorities in areas of employment, education, and culture from which they have been historically excluded by prohibiting discrimination on the basis of gender, race, color, and national origin in programs and activities receiving federal financial assistance. To varying degrees of success, affirmative action and, later, social equity projects under the banner of "multiculturalism" attempted to target the long and protracted history of institutional racism and sexism in the United States. It is no coincidence that Sotomayor's own educational trajectory roughly coincides with both the emergence and the decline of the social and educational policy initiatives that gave entry to women and underrepresented minorities in American higher education. First, the rise of affirmative action initiatives that emerged in the form of equity laws from President Johnson's vision of the Great Society—a society free of poverty and racism—had been implemented en masse when Sotomayor first arrived at Princeton in 1972 as a direct beneficiary of affirmative action; her class, for example, was only the third in Princeton's history to admit women as first-year students (Princeton first admitted women in 1969 but as transfer students from other colleges and universities). Second, her graduation from Yale Law School in 1979 also coincided with the steady decline of affirmative action at the national level at precisely the moment when multiculturalism began to emerge as a response to the waning of admissions based on race and gender quotas. Given the centrality of education to Sotomayor's own story, it would be useful to briefly highlight the decline of affirmative action and the subsequent emergence of multiculturalism as a well-intentioned, though largely unsuccessful, attempt to instantiate equality of opportunity in the ever-elusive pursuit of achieving the American dream of social and economic mobility through education.

Historical accounts of the policies associated with affirmative action often begin with President John F. Kennedy's Executive Order 10925 of 1961. Kennedy's order mandated the elimination of "racial discrimination in employment [because it injured] both its victims and the national economy." Quite simply, Kennedy's order required government contractors to "take *affirmative action* to ensure that applicants are employed and that employees are treated during employment without regard to their race, creed, color, or national origin" (my emphasis).[17] After Kennedy's assassination in 1963, President Johnson extended these mandates through the Civil Rights Act (1964) and with his own his own Executive Order 11246, which mandated that colleges and universities—especially, but certainly not exclusively, state-funded colleges and universities— extend to higher education what had been the legal standard in employment practices as overseen by the United States' Equal Employment Opportunity Commission.

Robert Fullinwider writes that "while the occasional court case and government initiative made the news and stirred some controversy, affirmative action was pretty far down the list of public excitements until the autumn of 1972," when it finally reached the hallowed halls of American colleges and universities. Though many elite colleges and universities had prepared for the eventuality of affirmative action after the passage of Civil Rights Act, the year 1972 marked the moment that "effected a change that punctured any [remaining] campus complacency" about the scope and reach of affirmative action.[18] As Fullinwider stresses, it is precisely at this moment in American history— when affirmative action reaches academia and begins to alter not just the racial makeup of the university but the economic access and rising success of minorities into the middle class—that we see the emergence of considerable controversy in public culture surrounding affirmative action's central tenets and prerogatives. Simply put, when affirmative action becomes successful it begins to be understood less as a corrective policy for past discriminations than as "preferential" treatment for some Americans at the expense of others.

This is not to suggest that Sotomayor was immune to the politics and controversies associated with affirmative action when she began studies at Princeton in 1972, or when she completed her studies at Yale Law School in 1979. Despite her phenomenal achievements at these two Ivy League universities, she did not have an easy time of it at these institutions. In *My Beloved World* she details one particularly harrowing experience at a recruiting dinner she attended with other Yale Law students on October 2, 1978. The dinner was sponsored by a Washington white-shoe law firm, then known as Shaw, Pittman, Potts & Trowbridge, as an opportunity for students to meet several of the firm's members in advance of more formal interviews that had been scheduled for the following day.[19] During the dinner, Martin Krall, a partner at the firm, asked Sotomayor a number of questions that took her aback. She relates how "as soon as the introductions were over, and before another word was spoken, the partner facing me [Krall] asked whether I believed in affirmative action. 'Yes,' I said, somewhat guarded but hardly imagining what my answer would unleash." Krall then proceeded to disingenuously bait Sotomayor, asking,

> "Do Princeton and Yale have affirmative action programs?" Yes, of course they do, I told him, at which the challenge only escalated: "Do you believe law firms should practice affirmative action? Don't you think it's a disservice to minorities, hiring them without the necessary credentials, knowing you'll have to fire them a few years later?"

He continued baiting a stunned Sotomayor: "But that's the problem with affirmative action. You have to wait to see if people are qualified or not. Do you think you would have been admitted to Yale Law School if you were not Puerto Rican?" The level of tension in the conversation became increasingly charged and acrimonious, as Sotomayor relates it. She nonetheless engaged Krall's provocations by refusing to understand his questioning of her abilities and, indeed, of her person, as a series of foregone rhetorical conclusions. As her adrenaline both rushed and ebbed, she responded calmly but firmly with the facts: "It probably didn't hurt.... But I imagine that graduating summa cum laude and Phi Beta Kappa from Princeton had something to do with it too."[20]

The abuse that Sotomayor was subjected to at the hands of a senior partner from a top Washington, DC, law firm recruiting at Yale Law seems unconscionable from our presentist vantage point. After all, any reasonable person would expect a Yale Law graduate such as Krall (class of 1965) to know the difference between provocative race-baiting and an earnest discussion about the policies and practices of affirmative action in 1978. Sotomayor's experience that fall, just a year before she was to graduate from Yale Law in 1979, is perhaps emblematic of the cultural shift in the country regarding the ostensible benefits and limits of affirmative action as a broad-scale corrective to disenfranchisement through education. It is perhaps not coincidental that 1978 also marked the beginning of the end for affirmative action (as it had been implemented when Sotomayor arrived at Princeton) after it was effectively diminished by the Supreme Court case, *Regents of the University of California v. Bakke* (1978).[21] The *Bakke* case stacked the deck against affirmative action less than fourteen years after the passage of the Civil Rights Act of 1964 and the various executive orders that sought to counter the institutionalization of discrimination against racialized minorities and women in both the labor force and academic institutions. In academia, for example, the policies associated with affirmative action had doubled the number of Blacks attending college and tripled the number of women on campuses throughout the country up to the *Bakke* case. Despite the marked success of affirmative action for Blacks, it should be noted that Anglo-American women were the primary beneficiaries of affirmative action; their progress simply "outpaced all minority men and women in every sector."[22] Though anti–affirmative action sentiment had been building in conservative media, in venues such as the ultraconservative *National Review,* then headed by the Republican ideologue and Yale graduate William F. Buckley Jr. (1925–2008), the *Bakke* case began to publicly cohere around the unfounded belief that racialized minorities were given a proverbial "free ride" at the expense of qualified white men and women. The legacy of the *Bakke* case forms the basis of what is now left of affirmative action, and that legacy is essential to understanding Sotomayor's relationship to affirmative action as well as its afterlives—especially after the emergence of multiculturalism in the 1980s.

The *Bakke* case reached the Supreme Court after Allan Paul Bakke (1940–), a thirty-three-year-old white man at the time, had twice applied for admission to the University of California, Davis, Medical School and had twice been rejected. As Christopher Newfield has noted regarding the significance of *Bakke,* the University of California, Davis's affirmative action program was no different from many others, "resting on the Civil Rights Act of 1964 and subsequent executive orders to act affirmatively to ensure equal treatment without regard to race. These measures did not mandate cross-racial equality of result, but they did erode the racially neutral yet disparity-producing mechanisms that had historically blocked such equality."[23] Newfield's admonition that affirmative action did not require "equality of result" puts into relief just how tenuous these polices actually were at remediating U.S. schools' long histories of failing to meet the needs of underrepresented groups. In this context, Sotomayor's indignation must be understood not just in relation to what she knew she had overcome in order to make it to Yale Law, but also in relation to what cultural elites like Krall believed, even beyond white-shoe law firms at the time, along with what they *felt* but could not always publicly share: that minorities largely do not deserve the benefits of affirmative action and are a detriment to "excellence."

As Krall put it in his ill-tempered attack on Sotomayor (whom he did not know at all until that frightful dinner reception), affirmative action had eroded the standard of excellence that had been the hallmark of top colleges and universities as soon as minorities arrived through that "special door." Though Krall appeared to be unencumbered by his own gross display of arrogance, not to mention prejudice, he was in effect asking Sotomayor to feel as if she herself were "a problem." The processes through which an individual is made to feel as if he is the manifestation incarnate of "a problem" was one of W. E. B. Du Bois's fundamental rhetorical insights proffered in the form of a question in *The Souls of Black Folks* (1903): "How does it feel to be a problem?" As noted in the introduction, when Du Bois asks his emblematic question and puts into stark relief the weight and waves of unrelenting national antagonisms against Blacks from enslavement to the emergence of Jim Crow laws, he sought an accounting of the affective register of discrimination and its toll not just on Blacks but on the national body politic, the very soul of the country. The sense of "double consciousness," or of being unduly aware of how others judge you based not on your actions or character but on the color of your skin through "ocular evidence," carried a heavy price for Du Bois insofar as it spoke to how the existence of Jim Crow laws were a form of psychic bondage. Perhaps more significantly, Du Bois's clarity allows us to understand how double consciousness functioned as a strategy of containing ostensibly "free" Blacks who were considered anathema to real democracy. Krall was in effect asking Sotomayor to carry the weight of what he understood to be affirmative action: a handout to the mostly underserving at the cost of an excellence unburdened by the nation's history. That it was white women who had benefited more from affirmative action than Blacks or Latinos is, of course, part of the whitewashing that creates easy scapegoats; it is a fact conveniently lost to Krall in his call for "excellence." And this gets to one of the fundamental ironies at the heart of affirmative action that the likes of Krall will likely never contemplate: for most of the country's history the nation's top institutions of higher learning all practiced the most effective form of affirmative action, that is, an unexamined quota system in which all students were male and white.

It might strike us as distinctly un-American to reward an individual for simply being born male, not to mention white, rather than for that individual's own merits or other admirable faculties. But it is nonetheless the most enduring facet of our national inheritance. Indeed, the still unresolved nature of Du Bois's formulation, when considered in light of the Latino question, speaks volumes about how far we have come and how much farther we need to go. Equally telling, however, is that Krall himself would rather forget, or ignore, that his own entry and eventual graduation from Yale Law would have been unheard of a generation before because of his Jewish background. Krall's slight against Sotomayor, as evinced by his intemperate questioning, should foreground for us just how much the wages of privilege too often require the concomitant historical amnesias that Nuyorican Sonia from the Bronx so brilliantly refused at that fateful dinner. Beyond her thoughtful response, Sotomayor filed a formal complaint against the law firm charging it with discrimination and formally requesting that Yale Law bar the Washington, DC, firm from recruiting on campus. A student-faculty tribunal found that the complaint warranted action and ordered the white-shoe firm to write a letter of apology. When the letter arrived, the tribunal rejected it on the grounds that it did not address the implications or consequences of Krall's unexamined ignorance sufficiently. Sotomayor and the university eventually received another, more satisfactory letter.

Sotomayor's experience with Krall demonstrates how rectifying prejudicial treatment is ultimately contingent on laws that may not ever change the aggressors' hearts and minds—whether or not they themselves believe they are acting out of animus—but that are nonetheless necessary to prevent an individual's personal prejudice from becoming institutionalized. The degree of access and support that Sotomayor received from affirmative action's "special door," as she called it in her memoir, from the moment she first arrived at Princeton, to the resolution she was entitled to after the recruiting debacle at Yale Law, are no longer as clearly safeguarded, and the *Bakke* case is at the heart of that reality.

In 1978, just a year before Sotomayor graduated from Yale Law, the *Bakke* case was decided in a split decision by the Supreme Court. Four justices chose to address only the statutory issue of Title VI of the Civil Rights Act of 1964 and found for Bakke, including his admission to the medical school, because it determined that the quota in the university's admission plan had excluded him on the basis of his race (Bakke was one of 2,664 applicants that year for only one hundred places). At the educational level, Title VI of the Civil Rights Act prohibited discrimination on the basis of race, color, and national origin in programs and activities receiving federal financial assistance and had been the standard on most educational diversity initiatives and hiring protocols. Four other justices addressed the larger constitutional issue of the Equal Protection Clause, or the Constitution's Fourteenth Amendment, which prevents states from denying persons within their jurisdictions the equal protection of their laws. They found for the medical school because its intent was not to exclude Bakke but only to include individuals of other races for compelling government reasons. The deciding swing vote in *Bakke* was cast by Justice Lewis F. Powell Jr. (1907–1998), who stunningly found for both Bakke and the

University of California. And that finding is what has been at the heart of affirmative action disputes well into our present.

Associate Justice Powell's contention was that the Title VI provision of the Civil Rights Act was correct insofar that the University of California, Davis, had violated the "plain meaning" of the Civil Rights Act, which simply saw discrimination, as interpreted by him, as based on racial discrimination, even if Bakke was "white." Therefore—irrespective of historical context—the court ordered that Bakke be admitted to the medical school. Powell, however, was a genteel southern aristocrat of sorts who had been considered a racial moderate early in his career when he served as chair of the Richmond, Virginia, school board at the height of massive resistance to school desegregation in the state's capital after *Brown v. Board of Education* (1954). Perhaps owing to these experiences in Richmond, Powell found that the university could in fact use "race-conscious" factors in selecting its applicants to achieve the benefits of a "diverse student body." Again Newfield: "Powell in effect de-raced diversity" insofar as the *Bakke* decision did not protect the rights of groups that had been discriminated against but rather "the right of the university to run itself as it saw fit."[24] Powell's emphasis on the question of "diversity" signaled the now generalized consensus— from admissions practice to employment and beyond—that racial discrimination is wrong, but it did so by divorcing discrimination from the historical context that had made affirmative action necessary in the first place. The emphasis on managerial "diversity," that is, on how an educational institution or an employer can take racial differences into account as it sees fit, grew as disenfranchised groups' right to restrict the institutionalization of exclusion diminished in practice. After *Bakke*, the Supreme Court began to retreat from the "disparate impact" calculus for discrimination that construed Title VII of the Civil Rights Act as forbidding not only overt discrimination but also practices that are legal but discriminatory.[25] Justice Powell's *Bakke* decision has since become the basis for understanding the "legality" of what remains of affirmative action programs in our present. The major Supreme Court cases that have ruled on affirmative action after *Bakke*—most notably *Grutter v. Bollinger* (2003), *Fisher v. University of Texas* (2013, 2016), and *Schuette v. Coalition to Defend Affirmative Action* (2014)—have left intact the *Bakke* case's formula for prohibiting quotas while reaffirming universities' managerial role in taking race into account as they see fit and, in the *Schuette* decision, the right of citizens to disregard race altogether in college and university admissions.

Sotomayor's unpleasant interactions with Krall would, of course, still seem unimaginable today, but only insofar as she had recourse to protections in 1978 that she would not be able to count on now. Sotomayor, after all, made it to Princeton and succeeded as the result of an imperfect quota system that nonetheless allowed her incalculable drive and intelligence to thrive in ways otherwise immeasurable through the traditional university admissions calculus. As the more rigorous accounting of the disparate impact on minorities began to wane after the *Bakke* case, "multiculturalism" emerged in educational settings and the cultural sphere as a potential remedy to affirmative action's decline.

SOTOMAYOR AND THE ENDS OF MULTICULTURALISM

Though multiculturalism in the United States can be traced to American pragmatist thought in the work of thinkers as diverse as Du Bois (1868–1963) and John Dewey (1859–1952), the institutionalization of multiculturalism coalesces in the 1980s after *Bakke* as both an educational and cultural movement. It extended the civil rights battles of the late 1960s and the 1970s, which sought to find a common ground for envisioning a just American society that would not discriminate on the basis of race, ethnicity, class, religion, gender, or, later, sexual orientation. By the 1980s the practice of multiculturalism had been enshrined in educational settings and represented the understanding that racial, cultural, ethnic, and linguistic difference could and should coexist with majority conceptions of civic belonging.[26] Its emergence effectively institutionalized "positive affirmation" as "affirmative action" proper lost it grounding as a legal corrective to a national history of race-based discrimination and structural disenfranchisement. At its best, multicultural practice therefore represented a pedagogical and a culturally affirming response to a history of minority discrimination that had butted against the legacies of affirmative action's decline after *Bakke*. Multicultural and cultural pluralists' educational perspectives all sought to reaffirm the ostensible American democratic imperative of inclusion characterized by the unifying dictum *e pluribus unum* (out of many, one), or the belief in a cohesive nation whose strengths reside in the diversity of its people. These educational imperatives and public policy initiatives under the banner of multiculturalism after *Bakke* sought to remedy in the cultural sphere a history of national inequality by affirming, if not students' right to educational equity, at least the right to affirm cultural differences as well as ethnic and racial pride. While one cannot speak of a single hegemonic definition of "multiculturalism," since its definition has always been contingent on the various meanings ascribed to it by both its detractors and adherents, we can say that at its core the aim of multiculturalism was to create a fair-minded society that provided routes to socioeconomic mobility and cultural integration, especially through education.[27] Those who undertook cultural-pluralist initiatives in educational settings, and later in corporate America, understood that the task of achieving a more inclusive and tolerant society required the recognition that diverse national cultures cannot simply be assimilated into the cultural traditions of any one dominant group, regardless of how powerful that dominant group is at any historical moment, without a profound cost to both the aspiring minority and the ostensible largesse of the majority. But multicultural and cultural-pluralist initiatives that emphasized the unifying promise behind the national aphorism "out of many, one," did not survive the so-called culture wars of the late 1980s and early 1990s. The political bellwether state of California served again as the template for understanding the demise of affirmative action after *Bakke* and, not coincidentally, the concomitant waning of multiculturalism that bookended Sotomayor's arrival at Princeton in 1972 and her graduation from Yale Law in 1979.

The waves of discriminatory legislation in California, the most populous state in the country, not only became commonplace throughout the nation but also began to frame the succinct and telling story of the end of multiculturalism in the United States. Some of the most notable of these legislative initiatives were directed against what remained of affirmative action after *Bakke*. These initiatives included California's Proposition 187, which was introduced in 1994 to deny health care, public education, and state services to undocumented immigrants. The passage of Proposition 187—also known as the Save Our State Proposition and the SOS Proposition—constituted the first time in the nation that a state passed immigration legislation in what had been the constitutional provenance of the federal government.[28]

Though it was ultimately found unconstitutional by a federal court in 1997, its ultimate success rested on providing the blueprint for anti-Latino immigrant initiatives and tactics that were adopted by legislators throughout the nation.

On the heels of the extrajuridical success of Prop 187, California voters also passed one of the most significant assaults on affirmative action with the passage of the state's controversial Proposition 209 in 1996. Introduced by its proponents, without a sense of irony, as the California Civil Rights Initiative, Proposition 209 outlawed "preferential treatment" based on race, color, ethnicity, or national origin by amending the California Constitution to prohibit state institutions from considering race, sex, or ethnicity in the areas of public employment, public contracting, and public education.[29] The measure passed with resounding popular support, to the shock of progressives (many voters assumed it promoted equality of access, given the use of "Civil Rights" in the Proposition's naming strategy), and it ultimately signaled the arrival of the commonplace that the emphasis on race itself was "the problem." The passage of Proposition 209 also initiated the use of civil rights language turned against the very communities that had demanded equality of opportunity in the democratic commons. With the arrival of "color blindness," the "postrace" triumph of aesthetic inclusion over tangible enfranchisement, and the rise of multiculturalism's "positive affirmation" over affirmative action proper, Proposition 209 effectively neutralized the language of social justice by turning its precepts on its head through cynical appropriation. Not inconsequentially, as Lani Guinier and Gerald Torres have pointed out, the very year Proposition 209 is enshrined into the state constitution, California tellingly begins investing in "building more prisons than colleges."[30] Two years after the passage of Proposition 209, the question of language itself was at the heart of yet another educational debate in California. The normative assumptions undergirding nativists' beliefs in the supremacy of the English language in educational settings found unqualified expression with the passage of Proposition 227 in 1998. Proposition 227 mandated English as the only language of instruction in the state's public schools and effectively eliminated bilingual education. In the process it also further debilitated the already-weak link to social mobility through education that has been the hallmark of the American dream narrative of economic enfranchisement through schooling. These assaults on Latino civic enfranchisement enacted in California have continued well into our present and have spread throughout the country. If this seems like an overstatement, it is essential to at least gloss the depth of its reach.

Beyond the House bills, redacted history textbooks, and legalized profiling of Latinos discussed in chapter 1, educational and literal assaults on Latinos and Blacks have been unrelenting and are ultimately succeeding in casting Anglo-Americans as the victims of discrimination. In Virginia, the Project on Fair Representation (POFR), a designated nonprofit "public charity," launched websites in 2014 to recruit applicants rejected from Harvard University, the University of Wisconsin, and the University of North Carolina at Chapel Hill, in order to file lawsuits on their behalf in an effort to achieve the "fair representation" of whites and "real hard-working students," such as "model minority" Asian American students, in university and college admissions practices (see author website, figure 3).[31] Though the central focus of this group is the ostensible elimination "race" and "ethnicity" in college and university admissions, so that Anglo-Americans can continue to benefit as they have historically in this country, it also seeks to eliminate the vestiges of the Voting Rights Act of 1965 in order to reform "those provisions of the Voting Rights Act and other laws that encourage and mandate the creation of racially gerrymandered voting districts." Within this logic of white racial grievance, discriminatory educational practices and "gerrymandering" are the sole provenance of Latinos and Blacks, who make whites and "model minority" students suffer under what the POFR understands to be regimes of racial oppression. All these initiatives, propositions, and laws have called into question common notions about the nature of national belonging as they had been enacted through civil rights legislation and affirmative action policies. These legal assaults have succeeded in further debilitating the nation's historically second-class citizens, as well as aspirants to citizenship, from their already tenuous link to the American dream.

As I noted in chapter 1, it is only in this climate that, for example, former Heritage Foundation senior policy analyst Jason Richwine could claim that Latinos are simply inferior to what he calls the nation's Anglo-American "founding stock." Out of this cultural climate emerge grim statistics: Latinos experience "a higher rate of violent hate crime victimization than non-Hispanic whites."[32] Anti-Latino laws, initiatives, and cultural scapegoating have had a chilling effect on the nature of national belonging; they are destroying the dream of progress and social mobility, not just for Latino citizens and cultural citizens but for all Americans. From affirmative action as a legal corrective for the disenfranchised to the "positive affirmation" of a deracinated multiculturalism, we are left to ponder just who ultimately benefits from the demise, if not the outright obsolescence, of the American dream. Yet how can this be possible? Are we not a nation forging true equality as evidenced by the election and eventual reelection of the nation's first Black president, and the arrival of the Supreme Court's first Latina associate justice?

OCULAR EVIDENCE AND THE POSTRACE AESTHETIC

Critical legal theorist Sumi Cho defines "postracialism" as "a twenty-first-century ideology that reflects a belief that due to the significant racial progress that has been made, the state need not engage in race-based decision-making or adopt race-based remedies, and that civil society should eschew race as a central organizing principle of social action."[33] Cho explains that the postrace moment erroneously holds that conversations about race are irrelevant, and those who wish to discuss race are seen as divisive and destructive of hard-fought social gains. As Cho's definition makes clear, attending to the current logic of postracialism simply makes the analysis and critique of race passé. More importantly, it absolves majority cultural and institutional actors of their responsibility for past and present racism, not to mention for the erasure of the histories of legal correctives that sought to create a stronger, more resilient, and equitable America through perfectible democratic practice. It is now clear from our present vantage point that one of the unintended consequences of multiculturalism was the belief that merely making diversity visible through what I am here calling "ocular evidence" would somehow be sufficient to counter the heavy hand of broad discriminatory practices that only three decades ago would have seemed improbable if not outright unconscionable.

Vijay Prashad goes so far as to suggest that multiculturalism ultimately failed in the United States on the night of November

4, 2008, when Barack Obama walked onstage at Chicago's Grant Park and accepted the mantle of the presidency. "An epoch that opened up in the 1980s came to an end," Prashad writes, adding, "The day of the glass ceiling [was] now over," but not racism.[34] For Prashad, the arrival of a "postrace" epoch ushered in by Obama's reelection after multiculturalism's demise has been merely cosmetic or, if one prefers, an example of the triumph of political aesthetics over grounded political reality. The lessons learned after the demise of affirmative action post-*Bakke,* and the rise of multiculturalism in its wake, are now clearer than ever. The multicultural practice of "positive affirmation" and the celebration of difference at the expense of legally mandated inclusion now seem like a cruel ruse. Cultural affirmation projects, however well intentioned, are no substitute for the force of the law in its ability to counter historical and institutional discrimination. In light of this, I would like to suggest that this postrace narrative has also ushered in what we might call an attendant "postrace aesthetic" in which, for example, the success of exceptional minority figures—such as Obama or Sotomayor—serves as "proof" that race no longer matters in American civic life given their visibility in the public sphere. But blinders, if not ethical blindness, do not serve democratic practice. Such are the vagaries of ocular evidence and the wages of historical amnesias.

Cultural transpositions such as these uncritically privilege high-profile minorities such as Obama or Sotomayor as "visual evidence" incarnate of national racial and ethnic inclusion above and against the broader historical evidence of deep structural inequality for underrepresented groups in the country. This "color blindness" in contemporary postracial liberalism ignores the evidence at hand and reifies a nonexistent postrace ideal that paradoxically benefits whites anew at the expense of those whose lives are marked by daily encounters with structural racism. Indeed, early in his presidency, Obama's own postrace liberalism espoused a meritocratic imperative that purportedly understood the labor market and the economy to be so egalitarian as to be completely color-blind:

> The best thing that I can do for the African-American community or the Latino community or the Asian community is to get the economy as a whole moving. If I don't do that ... then I'm not going to be able to help anybody. So that's priority number one.[35]

Such economic color blindness on Obama's part can itself be read as a racial ideology that refuses to see race-based inequality in historical dimension. If color blindness purports that the best way to end discrimination is to "see" not race but only one's commonality with others, then it is tantamount to denying that poverty—and education as the principal means through which to leave it behind—is overwhelmingly still correlated with race in the United States. And this is surprising, especially for a president who has been well versed in civil rights history and who has taught antidiscrimination law, steeped as it is in scholarly literature on race, inequality, and their relationship with poverty. As Eduardo Bonilla-Silva has shown, a new racism emerges shielded by the logic of color blindness through ocular "evidence," in which "whites are allowed express resentment toward minorities; criticize their morality, values, and work ethic; and even claim to be the victims of 'reverse racism.'"[36] In the post–Jim Crow era, the success of this new racism depends not just on institutional white racial privilege but on model racialized minorities who can extol the benefits of the demise of the color line. Paradoxically, when the president refuses to see the links between race and access to wealth, he synecdochically serves as "proof" that racism is a bygone problem, as "evidenced" in figurations of a president who happens to be Black and in the exemplary life story of a Supreme Court associate justice who happens to be a Latina.

Tim Wise, in his *Colorblind: The Rise of Post-racial Politics and the Retreat from Racial Equity* (2010), provides a useful analogue to Obama's insistence on the economy's color blindness. He writes,

> Imagine how absurd it would be to say that universal programs of opportunity were the best solution for persons who were disabled. Since persons with disabilities face obstacles that are directly related to their disability ... to think that economic growth alone, or a jobs bill, or universal health care would suffice to remedy their social disempowerment would be preposterous.[37]

Following Wise's critique and despite our postrace aesthetic moment—in which the appearance of difference serves as the presumptive stand-in for equality of opportunity for all—anti-Latino initiatives and the profound cultural amnesia that subtend them all bump up against an undeniable contradiction between claims regarding a postrace America and another national reality in which anti-Latino racism and sentiment carry the institutional force of law well into the twenty-first century. Like the former president who nominated her, Sotomayor also functions as a figure of color blindness who purportedly stands to trump the historical record.

THE SOTOMAYOR EFFECT

The "Sotomayor effect," the belief that if she could achieve success, so can any other disenfranchised minority, along with her rise to the pinnacle of American civic life as evidence of a postracial moment, simply bears little relation to the educational reality for Latinos or to their standing in the nation's hierarchy. Indeed, the statistics are grim: Latinos are three times more likely to have an arrest record than a college diploma.[38] Educational researchers Patricia Gándara and Frances Contreras have parsed the Latino education crisis in sobering terms.[39] They write,

> Today the most urgent challenge for the American educational system has a Latino face. Latinos are the largest and most rapidly growing ethnic minority in the country, but academically, they are lagging dangerously far behind. As has been thoroughly documented, a college degree is increasingly a prerequisite for a middle-class job and middle-class income.... But about half of all Latino students fail even to graduate from high school, and while other ethnic groups—including African Americans—have gradually increased their graduation rates, Latinos have seen almost no such progress.[40]

Gándara and Contreras go so far as to assert that the Latino educational equity gap constitutes the nation's greatest "looming social and economic disaster."[41] Such an assessment places Latinos front and center in the country's educational crisis. The crisis proportions of the Latino educational equity gap are staggering and have profound implications for the nation's current and future workforce, not to mention the U.S. economy. An era in which education delimits what most Latinos and Blacks can accomplish in the world is an era that runs counter to democratic practice. If this seems like hyperbole, then let us briefly consider the most extensive recent study on student achievement and educational equity undertaken in the country to date.

Anthony P. Carnevale and Jeff Strohl add further nuance to the educational picture for Latino students that Gándara and

Contreras elucidated in their foundational study. The Carnevale and Strohl study emphasizes that in those instances when Latino and Black students *do* make it to college, they are essentially segregated from wealthier Anglo-Americans who go on to attend the nation's elite institutions. In their study, Carnevale and Strohl assert that "the American postsecondary system is a dual system of racially separate and unequal institutions despite the growing access of minorities to the postsecondary system." They continue,

> Polarization by race and ethnicity in the nation's postsecondary system has become the capstone for K-12 inequality and the complex economic and social mechanisms that create it. The postsecondary system mimics and magnifies the racial and ethnic inequality in educational preparation it inherits from the K-12.... The education system is colorblind in theory. In fact, it operates, at least in part, as a systematic barrier to college for many minorities who finish high school unprepared for college. It also limits college and career opportunities for many African Americans and Hispanics who are well prepared for higher education but tracked into crowded and underfunded colleges where they are less likely to develop fully or to graduate.[42]

Their study further demonstrated that since 2004 a larger proportion of students from high-income homes have enjoyed the benefits of wealthy elite colleges, while students from low-income backgrounds have been increasingly concentrated in poorer non-selective two- and four-year colleges that have lower completion rates, even though these students' academic ability is equal to that of students from more privileged socioeconomic backgrounds who go on to attend the nation's top colleges and universities. Latino and Black students in the study who scored just as high or higher than wealthier Anglo-American students on the SAT and

ACT college admissions tests were routinely funneled into the category of open-access "less- and noncompetitive" colleges and universities. Latino and Black students "not only have less access to postsecondary education in general, but in addition less access to the 468 elite colleges, less access to Bachelor's degrees, and less access to graduate degrees."[43] As the study makes clear, "minority" Latino and Black students from lower socioeconomic backgrounds who scored as high or higher than their Anglo-American counterparts on standard achievement tests are funneled into less competitive or noncompetitive colleges, where they are less likely to graduate than their lower-achieving but wealthier Anglo-American counterparts. Put another way, the educational outcomes of students reflect parental wealth, not their scores on traditional aptitude tests such as the SAT and the ACT. The implications for Latino and Black social mobility through education are clear and disarming: the educational system, once the social leveler of the civil rights era, is now perpetuating the class divide along economic lines correlated to race and ethnicity.

As Carnevale and Strohl have unequivocally demonstrated, what we have is a tiered, caste-like educational system, not educational equity. Those who begin with economic disadvantages are increasingly unlikely to cross class divides. As the current research about Latino and Black educational access makes clear—form Gándara and Contreras to Carnevale and Strohl—the demographic picture for Latino and Black student educational success is bleak. And it bears no resemblance to Sotomayor's exceptional story of educational achievement. Given the institutionalized educational divestment of Latinos from the fiber of American public life, not to mention its relationship to Black civil rights, it behooves us to understand why Sotomayor's American dream story of economic and social mobility has been so historically elusive for so many Americans and for Latinos most particularly.

Ignoring that Latinos and Latinas are historically the least likely to graduate from high school, much less college, dooms too many aspirants to the success that Sotomayor's story promises to resounding failure unless we learn to distinguish real inclusion from the limits of symbolic inclusion. But most importantly, ignoring this distinction absolves our national institutions from accounting why our democracy has failed such a demographically significant component of the American body politic. The juridical principle of *inclusio unius est exclusio alterius,* that is, "to include one is to exclude the others," is resonant here. Sotomayor represents an exceptional Latina life story because most Latinos have been systematically denied the inclusion that underwrites her uplifting story of educational achievement and human resiliency, laying bare what we might call "the Sotomayor effect": the spectacular success of a representative figure that paradoxically obscures the reality of exclusion for disenfranchised scores of Americans in lived historical and institutional practice. Her very exceptionalism requires that we understand anything less as a question of personal deficiency rather than limited individual agency in the face of institutionalized divestment. Sotomayor's success is spectacular precisely because she is the exception that proves the rule of Latinos' national exclusion. She becomes, paradoxically, a spectacular Latina because she earns our collective national sympathy by overcoming adversity, as if, somehow, Latinos must be necessarily tested and burdened—a priori—with the need to prove their humanity before being embraced by the very systems of exclusion that deny them access to education. Given the complexities of the Latino question, just how far can a story of talent and the vagaries of circumstances elevate one person to become the representative surrogate for over 57.5 million "others"?

When we examine the Sotomayor effect in our historical moment, when we substitute the symbol of inclusion for the complex story it purportedly represents, we come to realize that the Latino question is far from answered, nor even understood. What is more, we may even begin to break from the elusive embrace of a spectacular image we wish to believe in against all evidence to the contrary. Though that evidence is all around us, it is tempting nonetheless to understand this rhetorical substitution as proof of an unprecedented postracial shift from institutional and national exclusion to the incorporation and assimilation of Latinos writ large. But limited educational opportunities, the rejection of laws to redress racial subordination, a broken immigration system, and the scapegoating of Latinos, as well as the disavowal of Latino history, all put the lie to the much-exaggerated entry of the Latino body into American civic life.

We must ask ourselves, why are stories of Latino inclusion in the American body politic so important to us? Who benefits from the perpetuation of such stories in a purportedly postracial and color-blind moment? Can Sotomayor allow us to reinvent the American dream through sheer example and inspiration? Can her rise be seen as a sign, however tenuous, of the country's progress on the Latino question? What can Latinos and all Americans learn from Sotomayor's story of studied dedication in the face of insurmountable odds? So it is to that paradox of inclusion in our purportedly postracial moment—"the Sotomayor effect" against the evidence before us—that I now turn.

PART II

Losing Sonia Sotomayor

Fascism sees its salvation in giving [the] masses not their right, but instead a chance to express themselves.

Walter Benjamin, "The Work of Art in the Age of Its Technological Reproduction" (1936)

CHAPTER THREE

Sonia Sotomayor, the Mediapheme

When Sonia was nine, her father passed away.... Her mother worked six days a week as a nurse to provide for Sonia and her brother.... With the support of family, friends, and teachers, Sonia earned scholarships to Princeton, where she graduated at the top of her class, and Yale Law School, where she was an editor of the *Yale Law Journal,* stepping onto the path that led her here today. Along the way she's faced down barriers, overcome the odds, lived out the American dream that brought her parents here so long ago. And even as she has accomplished so much in her life, she has never forgotten where she began, never lost touch with the community that supported her. What Sonia will bring to the Court, then, is not only the knowledge and experience acquired over a course of a brilliant legal career, but the wisdom accumulated from an inspiring life's journey.... Well, Sonia, what you've shown in your life is that it doesn't matter where you come from, what you look like, or what challenges life throws your way—no dream is beyond reach in the United States of America.

Barack Obama[1]

President Obama's nomination of Sonia Sotomayor to the Supreme Court seemed to confirm that as a country we were truly experiencing a postrace transformation and a series of symbolic "firsts": the nation's first Black president nominating the first Latina to the nation's highest court. Given the paucity of Latino participation in American history and institutions, Sotomayor's nomination seemed to signal a blow to a protracted history of Latino and minority disenfranchisement from the national culture. Not surprisingly, when Obama introduced her as his nominee to replace retiring associate justice David Souter (1939–), he did so in a way that couched her life story within the emplotments of an American dream that resonated with both those who needed to believe in its promise in the middle of an economic crisis, and with those in consort with the version of individualism—the "bootstraps" narrative I noted in chapter 2—touted by conservative ideologues. The president was prosaic in this regard as he further described Sotomayor's life and educational trajectory to a televised audience in what was the first Supreme Court nomination to be streamed live on the internet. He summarized his nominating speech by resorting to a commonplace conceit, albeit with characteristic oratorical flare: "With a good education here in America, all things are possible."

Like many who saw the live televised event, heard it on the radio, or watched it on the internet, the excitement drowned many of the factual inaccuracies in the president's speech, such as when he stated that it was "the American dream that *brought her parents here* so long ago" (my emphasis). Since Puerto Ricans are U.S. citizens by birth, this "here," this America, seemed like an oddly imprecise, if not altogether ahistorical, characterization of her parent's migration from Puerto Rico to New York City. However imprecise, it certainly fit seamlessly into the

American dream romance the president himself had offered the nation in his own memoir, *Dreams of My Father* (1995), when he was preparing to launch his own political campaign to become an Illinois senator.[2] Packaged anew for Sotomayor at the time, Obama's soundbite, his branded message of hope—"in America, all things are possible"—garnered considerable traction in the public imagination as it was repeated in various news loops and was plaintively stated by Sotomayor herself during her Senate confirmation hearings:

> The progression of my life has been uniquely American.... My father, a factory worker with a third-grade education, passed away when I was 9 years old. On her own, my mother raised my brother and me. She taught us that the key to success in America is a good education. And she set the example, studying alongside my brother and me at our kitchen table so she could become a registered nurse. We worked hard.[3]

Sotomayor's telling of her life story read like a page from the national multicultural storybook of inclusion as rendered and made possible by the American dream. Yet its invocation in political language, by both Obama and Sotomayor herself, also evinced a willing rebranding of the American dream precisely at a moment when Americans were beginning to understand it as an unattainable cynical fiction. Anyone buoyed by her message of laboring toward the benefits of social mobility that day in June 2009 likely did not know that anyone working full time on minimum wage would simply be unable to survive on $5.15 an hour. As we saw in chapter 2, the American dream, beyond its positive connotations in the public imagination, has been submitted to considerable scrutiny by political theorists and cultural historians as much for what it promises ("in America, all things are possible") as for its subtending fictions. Indeed, Sotomayor's tale of sacrifice and her

parents *immigration*—later described as colonial *migration* from
Puerto Rico in her memoir—was presented alongside anecdotes
of how study, determination, and diligence served as the necessary antidotes to overcoming poverty, language barriers, and discrimination in an America where social mobility was possible
through education and the sheer will to succeed. It is undoubtedly
a valuable and intimately political story of American exceptionalism with a familiar narrative arc of upward mobility that
Sotomayor later expanded in her best-selling memoir, *My Beloved
World,* for which she has earned over $2.5 million and counting.[4]
The message branded by the White House through various media
ultimately succeeded by exalting, first, Sotomayor's humble ethnic origins and then, paradoxically, by assuring the nation that she
would apply the "rule of law" *despite* her ethnic particularisms. It
represented the triumph of a strategic and highly readable nationalist biography that was emblematic of American values over and
beyond anything remotely resembling ideology or the intellectual rigor associated with ideological conviction.

Sotomayor's nomination and eventual confirmation were, of
course, momentous. Supreme Court justices are appointed by
presidents and—like Federal Reserve Board appointees—stand to
leave an enduring, indelible mark on American civic life even
beyond the term limits of the president who nominates them. And
that has certainly been the case with Sotomayor. Her ability to
reach various constituencies by walking that fine line between ethnic subject and color-blind defender of the rule of law has made
her the best-known justice in the country, if not the world. Not
surprisingly, after her confirmation, Sotomayor began to be
admired in a way that is intelligible in contemporary American
culture by making her represent not just the elusive fulfillment of
an all too exhausted "American dream" but its fulfillment *as* an

ethnic subject: a representative Latina. One of the defining features of this most recent incarnation of the American narrative of social mobility and assimilation—the American dream after multiculturalism I described earlier—is an insistence on reifying ethnic difference as an aesthetic category outside history. As I've noted, multiculturalism has been largely transformed from a corrective for the benefit of disenfranchised groups after the end of affirmative action up to the *Bakke* case into what might be best described as aesthetic inclusion without the legal scaffolding to make inclusion meaningful. This aesthetic multiculturalism marks new ways of seeing and perceiving the ethnically and racially marked subject in public culture. Assimilation becomes an aesthetic practice of absorption, ostensible integration in media campaigns, and glossy brochures but, ultimately, a performance of mimicry. Ethnic subjects' assimilation requires that they perform and adopt normative "nationalist" values and that they diffuse these values in their public personae, as in Sotomayor's adoption of an ethnically inflected American dream to explain both her success and the possibilities it ostensibly holds for others like her. It is a narrative of integration through assimilation that is as well worn as it is compelling. This is especially true in a moment of national instability such as ours, with torch-wielding neo-Nazis running roughshod over the veneer of Mr. Jefferson's University in Charlottesville, Virginia, and beyond. And it is also a narrative that fuels public policy priorities, laws, institutional practices, and, perhaps most significantly, our own national identity in alt-right times. In the process, the performance of inclusion begins to supplant political inclusion proper.

Coinciding with the first major assaults on affirmative action programs after *Bakke* and especially during President Ronald Reagan's ascendency—programs for whom the likes of Sotomayor had been the primary beneficiaries—the emergence of aesthetic multiculturalism began to enshrine the image of inclusion, and the attendant hope that sustains it, as the "measure of making it," in the absence of broader empirical evidence of inclusion on a national scale. If this seems like a harsh observation, let us reflect on the evidence at hand and how this has come to be after Trumpism.

REPRESENTATIVE PERSONHOOD
IN THE AGE OF ALTERNATIVE FACTS

> A representative man (or perhaps a representative woman)—to use the term that came into common usage in mid-nineteenth century America—was a person who encapsulated the highest aspirations of his racial or cultural group, in terms of education, professional advancement, and intellectual ability. The very existence of such persons was a potent argument for the inclusion of marginalized peoples in the larger fabric of American life.
>
> Kenneth W. Mack[5]

It would not be a stretch to concede that, next to Obama, Sotomayor is the most significant figure to emerge from the contemporary postracial narrative of American multicultural inclusion. She has become, in the language of political and media studies, a "mediapheme." Mediaphemes function as quick encapsulations of stories that are themselves proxies for particular histories. It is in this sense that the mediapheme is the most common unit of communication in mass-mediated modes of national mythmaking and remembering. The mediapheme tends to last as long as the person, story, issue, or event is newsworthy.[6] Once a person, story, or event is translated into mediaphemic form, it ricochets through channels of mass communication with ease. In the process, "the medium becomes the message" at the expense of the story it indexes. Unlike a political "soundbite," a mediapheme is a palimpsest of accumulated stories (visual, aural, or narrative), one that becomes a cultural shorthand for the more complex histories it references. The mediapheme enacts an indexical relationship to the person, cultural object, or story it references to the point that the truth-bearing qualities of the mediapheme can both exceed and delimit the reality it references. Put simply, the mediapheme is at once an object of cultural memory and, wittingly or not, a potential technology for historical forgetting and, worse, outright political misrepresentation and elision. In our alt-right, "alternative facts" moment, the mediapheme is the central vehicle for understanding how truth and related evidentiary protocols have given way to "alternative facts" and the rise of "fake news" and "deepfake" media. In an atmosphere of truth claims without the accounting to substantiate any given claim, the mediapheme becomes the stand-in for evidence unless it is either debunked or substituted. If it is not, it lingers as a memory of a once remembered "fact," alternative or otherwise. The afterlives of the mediapheme condition political feelings that are guarded against reflection or historical reckoning unless there is a demand to interrogate the mediapheme's truth claims or, as Stephen Colbert once remarked, its "truthiness."

President Trump is a masterful deceiver insofar as he knows that information is a commodity premised on individual prejudices, one that is to be exploited through the repetitive cycles of the mediaphemic loop's newest technology for casting the widest net imaginable for fabricating partial, half-, or untruths with unimaginable expediency: Twitter. Wittingly or not, Trump proved that Joseph Goebbels's old Nazi maxim is true in the era of Twitter: if you repeat a lie long and forcefully enough through mass channels of easily accessible communication, it becomes the truth to many (though, thankfully, not to all). Psychologists call this the "illusory truth effect," and in our era of alt-facts, these mediaphemes, or "truth effects," can take hold of the public imagination for at least two reasons. First, any untruth can circulate through mass-mediatic channels of communication at unheard-of speed and reach vast swaths of undiscerning, uneducated ears, eager to have their own prejudices confirmed. Former presidential hopeful Hillary R. Clinton, for example, uncharitably characterized this lot of undiscerning ears as Trump's "basket of deplorables." Doing so paradoxically infuriated both undiscerning ears (with ostensibly misogynist hearts: "Lock her up!") and liberal-leaning interlocutors who were at the time worried about appearing "uncivil" in the face of the public misinformation campaign that Trump was waging against everyone but the so-called deplorables. Unlike historical cycles of misinformation, the mediapheme now requires correctives from those who can parse truth from fiction with equal speed and are in a position to either counter the mediapheme or sit idly by. Leaving truth telling to the normative ethical and political proclivities of subjects is obviously problematic, not least because democratic practice requires a formidable fourth estate. The press, while historically central to democratic practice, has been under attack as never before in the country's history. When the mediapheme circulates through mass channels of communication with impunity, by the time the lie is sorted out—if it is sorted out—even the airing of the lie itself reinforce its "truth effect" to the very prejudices that undiscerning ears want confirmed. That is, given the continual lies and half-truths that characterize the current president and his administration, any serious consideration of his truth claims paradoxically and exponentially expands the potential for the lie to be taken as a truth guarded against reflection. Given its significance, it would be useful to elaborate how the use value of the Sotomayor mediapheme was interpreted by various constituencies and through various mass-mediated channels of communication to different contradictory and often antagonistic ends. The Sotomayor mediapheme can tell us a great deal about being Latino in the United States, as well as the promise and limits of representative personhood in a purportedly postracial moment. What can we learn about representative Latino personhood by understanding how the simulacrum of inclusion is conflated with political and civic incorporation proper?

The various versions of Sonia Sotomayor's life story enact wildly different relationships to the American body politic during one of the most significant demographic, racial, ethnic, linguistic, and information-driven transformations imaginable in the history of the United States. Given what demographers have called "the Latinization of the United States," and what others have called the Latino *reconquista,* it becomes imperative to understand the realignment of a social order that has yet to account for how over 57.5 million Latino bodies are largely absent from the national policy table and its attendant circuits of power. Whatever our political proclivities or cultural points of reference, Sotomayor has become a representative Latina.

Sotomayor is the most recent heir to a long tradition of national mythmaking inaugurated by Ralph Waldo Emerson. America, Emerson argued, needed "representative characters" who could serve as vehicles of education for the broader good of the democratic order. Emerson's *Representative Men* (1850) projected onto the American historical imagination characters from the Old World who would—like Plato, Goethe, and many others—provide exceptional models for the less-than-perfect union he saw before him after the end of the U.S.-Mexico War (1846–48). Emerson's heirs, such as Abraham Lincoln, Frederick Douglass, Martin Luther King Jr., John F. Kennedy, and many other representative characters known to schoolchildren, have been inscribed into the fiber of a broader American national civic pedagogy: didactic figures through whom the character and promise of American political life can be rearticulated at moments of national transformation, political strife, and crisis.

Elaborating on Emerson's "representative characters," the historian Kenneth W. Mack explains the use value of representative personhood in the struggle for the civic enfranchisement of Blacks in and through the practice of jurisprudence. In his deft *Representing the Race: The Creation of the Civil Rights Lawyer* (2012), Mack establishes the connection between Black representative figures in jurisprudence, such as the first Black Supreme Court justice, Thurgood Marshall (1908–93), as instrumental in the battle for Black incorporation into the American body politic. For Mack, "the representative Negro" was "the black person who crossed racial lines, and often shook up the expectations of a segregated society":

> It was an African American whose formative experience with race came in an encounter with segregated public space. It was also—on many occasions—a black person who was as unlike the rest of his race as possible. A segregated society often demanded that representative Negroes be racially ambiguous. But that society also demanded more. It required that they be authentic representatives of those who would never be allowed into Harvard ... or the Supreme Court's hallowed space. It was an experience fraught with deeply conflicted emotions and desires.[7]

Plotting Mack's description onto the Sotomayor mediapheme is useful. Mack's analysis of the Black representative figures who were central to the history of the civil rights movement holds that what they had in common—in addition to their race and the discrimination they endured because of it—is both the language and symbolic use value of the law as the key that provided entry into civic life. For them, jurisprudence was a profession of like-minded individuals who would interpret the law with the respect that established tradition required in order to expand the democratic commons. In other words, they were Black representative figures who were assimilable into the body politic by virtue of their respect for the law, a respect that would, in turn, augur well for their own incorporation and, by extension, the incorporation of other Blacks into the national fold. In Mack's study, what distinguishes Black representative figures such as Marshall from Sotomayor is that practicing law for those Black representative figures was, above and beyond the possibility of incorporation into civic life, the eventual and purposeful creation of laws that would facilitate the entry of all Blacks into full citizenship. One of the most significant of these legal battles was, of course, Marshall's victory as the NAACP chief counsel in *Brown v. Board of Education* (1954), which effectively ushered in the civil rights acts of the 1960s and the educational and political opportunities that followed through various executive orders. In an era when educational roadblocks and discrimination limit what most Latinos can accomplish, or even what they can imagine in the world, a representative Latina for the nation is certainly a potent symbol of inclusion. But what happens when the use value of the symbol remains in the realm of representation? More specifically, if Sotomayor represents the fulfillment of the American dream of inclusion for scores of Latinos and the broader body politic as, for example, Antonia Felix contends in her unambiguously titled hagiography of the justice, *Sonia*

Sotomayor: The True American Dream (2010), what are we to make of the evidence to the contrary? What are we to make of the scores of *lawfully* disenfranchised Latino bodies around us? This accounting is necessary when we consider the unraveling of the gains associated with the civil rights movement in the latter part of the twentieth century, as evidenced in the proliferation of anti–affirmative action lawsuits, voter-disenfranchisement initiatives, the caging of immigrant children at the border, the move to revoke U.S. citizenship from Latino citizens, and related rulings made by a deeply divided Supreme Court distrustful of the recognition of race as a category of analysis that might counter our era's purportedly "color-blind" justice. The "law" as a repairable and recoverable project toward justice, as it was understood by scores of Black activists, lawyers, and Marshall himself, is simply coming undone in ways that a generation ago would have been unthinkable. Enter Sonia Sotomayor. Sotomayor's use value to our national pedagogies and stories of inclusion provides a window through which we can see precisely how she is the exception to the rule. Meanwhile, the evidence of injustice around us compels us to make sense of the broader Latino question, as Latinos continue to be remanded to the orders of national abjection through law and historical disavowal.

BECOMING SONIA SOTOMAYOR

Like many Americans, and particularly as a scholar and teacher of U.S. Latino studies, I was moved by President Obama's speech nominating Sotomayor to the Supreme Court in 2009. Suddenly, it seemed that versions of Sotomayor's life story were reproduced in every medium imaginable. In Puerto Rico the local press could not have been more ecstatic that an "accomplished"

Puerto Rican outside the entertainment or sports industry was finally getting some recognition. Exuberant enthusiasm prevailed despite the island's more conservative commentators' insistence that she is not really a Puerto Rican. They often noted that she is a "Nuyorican," a Puerto Rican from New York. Even former Miss Puerto Rico Íngrid Marie Rivera (1983–) opined in no uncertain terms, and without irony, that the president's nomination proved that the island's women were not just beautiful but smart as well, as if beauty and brains were mutually exclusive qualities that could be conferred by no less an arbiter of both as Obama. I was most struck, however, by the profoundly misinformed and sensationalist reporting that emerged after the well worn "wise Latina" comment transformed Sotomayor, the person, into a media spectacle.

Sotomayor's "wise Latina" comment was made at the Judge Mario G. Olmos Law and Cultural Diversity Lecture at the University of California, Berkeley, in 2001. At the lecture, Sotomayor said,

> Justice [Sandra Day] O'Connor has often been cited as saying that a wise old man and wise old woman will reach the same conclusion in deciding cases.... I am not so sure that I agree with the statement. First ... there can never be a universal definition of wise. Second, I would hope that a wise Latina woman with the richness of her experiences would more often than not reach a better conclusion than a white male who hasn't lived that life.[8]

The conservative news media and blogosphere erupted with claims that this represented patent "reverse discrimination," while on the other side of the political spectrum there seemed to be an uncritical exuberance over the recognition that ethno-racial sensitivity and empathy should be part of a Supreme Court justice's repertoire. Sotomayor's "wise Latina" comment became the operative mediapheme though which to understand calls for or against her nomination. Histrionic radio talk show host Rush Limbaugh, along with former Republican House speaker and erstwhile presidential hopeful Newt Gingrich, rallied an army of Republican members of Congress and their constituents to express "deep concern" about Sotomayor's "blatant racism." Limbaugh chimed in with the usual hyperbole for which he is known: "Obama is the greatest living example of a reverse racist, and now he's appointed one ... to the U.S. Supreme Court.... We are confronting a radical assault on this nation, a radical assault today on the U.S. Supreme Court." Gingrich, who had famously called Obama "the food stamp president,"[9] chimed in almost immediately after the nomination: "White man racist nominee would be forced to withdraw. Latina woman racist nominee should also withdraw."[10] Gingrich and Limbaugh's early rejoinders to Obama's nomination of Sotomayor, and the interventions that followed by mostly conservative commentators, ironically cast both the first nonwhite president and the first Latina to be appointed to the U.S. Supreme Court as "racists." For commentators like Limbaugh, Gingrich, and those of their ilk, the state of racism in the United States simply constructed whites as the victims of "reverse discrimination." The perceived gains achieved through affirmative action by the president, his nominee, and presumably other minorities like them paradoxically impeded and infringed on the rights of the dominant Anglo-American white majority. This ahistorical whitewashing, unfettered by either facts or the larger society's quest for true democratic equality of access to opportunity, had the effect of trumping cause-effect relations by uncritically holding "reverse discrimination" as the fundamental culprit of white national suffering. If we have a Black president, how can we be

racists? One of the effects of the historical whitewashing surrounding the nomination of a Latina to the Supreme Court by a
Black president was the emergence of mass-mediated "alternative facts" and conspiracy theories about who she "really was."
The ad hominem attacks and resultant character assassination
in the mediasphere made reality ancillary to the individual versions of her story that rapidly circulated and gained traction
through the Twittersphere and blogosphere in ways unimaginable during previous confirmation hearings.

CONTRARIAN HISTORIES

After Sotomayor's nomination, Andy Martin (1945), a Tea
Party mouthpiece, birther conspiracy advocate, and self-pro-
fessed "right of the right internet activist," promised an exposé
of Sotomayor that would derail her confirmation. Martin is perhaps best known for his allegations that Obama is a Muslim and
for his spurious lawsuit against the state of Hawaii seeking to
verify the president's official birth certificate (allegations that
Trump himself used in his own demands that Obama prove he
was indeed born in the United States). He alleged that Sotomayor
had a secret agenda informed by her anti-American politics and
her "predatory sexuality." In a post provocatively entitled "Second Circuit Gossip: Sotomayor, 'Deeply-closeted' Lesbian Cougar," Martin asserted that the media and politicians who had
focused on Sotomayor's judicial decisions were looking in the
wrong place for insight into her character and disposition; her
true agenda was to be found in the secret details of her personal
life. Martin promised to offer evidence that Sotomayor was "a
deeply-closeted lesbian" who had previously been "in a 'sham'
marriage ... to conceal her sexual identity."[11] Martin's broader

concern was the prospect of an eventual gay marriage show-down at the Supreme Court and how Sotomayor's sexual "empa-thy" would ultimately destroy "the sacred institution" of hetero-sexual marriage. Indeed, Martin's version of Sotomayor's alleged secret life, reminiscent of Cold War red scare smear campaigns, has become part of Tea Party and birther lore about Obama's purported attempts to make a "Sodom and Gomorrah of our Capital" and "a sham of our Constitution" with the appointment of a divorced and childless Latina. Alleging that Sotomayor was a lesbian allowed Martin to recast a Latina success story as a life premised on falsehoods for his readers and sympathizers desir-ous of "evidence," however spurious, of a "deep state" ready to take over American institutions with the ascension of Black and Brown bodies to its founding institutions. In contrast, Justice Brett Kavanaugh verbally attacked Democratic members to the Senate Judiciary Committee during his confirmation hearings in a screed about how they were smearing him as no one had been smeared in the country's history. His protestations thus whitewashed all that Sotomayor had herself endured before and up to her hearings by the very supporters who sought to ensure his confirmation. Martin's specious conspiracy theories about Obama's birthplace and Sotomayor's sexuality lacked evidence but caused real harm.

It is consequential that "conspiracy theories" are now central to maintaining white supremacist ideologies. The Sotomayor mediapheme that circulated had at least three axes of attack. Alternately describing Sotomayor as a "reverse racist," a "lesbian cougar," or as too empathic for rational thought, the media-pheme used both the confluence of events and the necessary dissemination technologies at the time of her confirmation to produce the scaffolding that is now emblematic of our posttruth moment: through repeated circulation, the mediapheme takes on a life of its own. Sotomayor, perhaps too wise or too cunning for the national good in her ability to pass for a respectable, "real" American, was posited as an alien ready to overturn the social order through the imposition of perverted values foreign to the national character. Though one might describe such diatribes as fodder written by and for the unbalanced, the record shows that the lack of historical perspective was a central part of the Sotomayor mediapheme, as evidenced in various print and media outlets. What is clear from a distance is that Martin's fodder was meant to travel online through the media ecosystem until it become a headline that generated "real" adherents who repeated it and peddled it *as if* it were a secular gospel. While claims about her sexuality ultimately didn't stick, Sotomayor's purported empathy and foreignness as a representative Latina did crystallize in the mainstream media. The emergence of the Latino question during and after the confirmation hearings laid bare the problem with representative personhood for Latinos. The confirmation hearings thrust the Latino question into the forefront and made patent the extent of the conditions under which political enfranchisement can be either granted or denied to Latinos. Not least of which is the enduring conflation between Latinos of all national origins in the United States with "Mexicans," as Trump has done to destructive ends.

As a representative Latina, the mass-mediated Sotomayor who began to emerge became a palimpsest of competing truth claims about the nature of the ethnic subject's relation to social orders. Sotomayor's very intelligibility in the public sphere depended on presumptions about not just why a Latina would be certain to vote in a predictable way but about—on the strength of that presumption—why her nomination should be derailed a priori. Spurious attacks notwithstanding, and these were considerable, the Sotomayor mediapheme effectively evacuated her judicial record and, more importantly, the historical accounting required for a measured understanding of why her representative personhood, à la Emerson, should in fact matter greatly to an informed citizenry. In the bread-and-circuses zeitgeist created by the mediapheme, in which time, historical accounting, and facts became ancillary to the use value of "the event," it did not matter that Associate Justice Samuel Alito had made situated knowledge—what postmodernists used to call the question of "positionality"—central to his biographical narrative at his confirmation hearings in 1990.

Alito had explained that his ethnic background as the son of Italian immigrants gave him the empathy necessary to appreciate what other Supreme Court justices might not about immigration and the unfulfilled promise of American democratic inclusion. Alito noted that "when a case comes before me involving ... an immigrant—and we get an awful lot of immigration cases and naturalization cases—I can't help but think of my own ancestors, because it wasn't that long ago when they were in that position."[12] One might say that as "a wise Italian American," Alito was empathetic and that this was acceptable during his 1990 congressional confirmation hearings in a way that it was not in Sotomayor's. The Sotomayor mediapheme initially required a series of out-of-context rebuttals from the future associate justice that were replaced with her assertion during the confirmation hearings that the "wise Latina" comment was a "rhetorical flourish that fell flat ... [and] was bad."[13] Ultimately, her success at deflecting the "rhetorical flourish" that nearly derailed her confirmation came at a steep cost. She paradoxically had to disavow her sponsor, Obama, for strategic gain. Indeed, the defensive posture is what the mediapheme requires in an endless loop of resignification in which the classic narrative distinctions between story and discourse are made irrelevant: perception is made reality through the mediapheme's simulated reality. In ethnic studies, this process—through which one uses defensive postures to address misinformation and undo its damage—is referred to as "nonproductive labor." Nonproductive labor, simply put, is labor without speech. Taken from Karl Marx's inquiry into the nature of labor and alienation in his *Grundrisse* (1857–58)—"nonproductive labor" is what Marx called *Arbeit sans frase* (labor without speech). It describes the mechanisms through which laboring against a fallacy disengages cause from effect, an action from its purpose, and runs the risk making "story," the events as they happened from A to Z, indistinguishable from "discourse," the rearrangement of what really happened. In doing so it produces a version of reality that suits political purposes—what we used to call propaganda or agitprop and what we now call "alternative facts" in the age of mass-mediated assaults on reality.

The nonproductive labor that was required to qualify the "wise Latina" mediapheme, its endless redirects, and truncated explanations and disavowals, took away from conservatives and liberals alike the productive energy of speech directed to civic democratic ends. That is, had anyone bothered to look beyond the mediapheme, it would have been clear that Sotomayor was not exactly the empathetic "wise Latina" of the Berkeley diversity talk. For example, in the twenty-nine opinions Sotomayor wrote as a district and appeals court judge, she never once granted relief to a prisoner petitioning for a writ of habeas corpus, the appeal of last resort for the convicted.[14] During the confirmation hearings, Democratic senator Charles Schumer went so far as to remind the twenty-eight Republican senators who were opposing her nomination that she was a good nominee because her record actually represented a conservative bias. Without a hint of irony, Schumer flatly told the opposing GOP senators,

> She agreed with your Republican colleagues 95 percent of the time; she has ruled for the government in 83 percent of immigration cases; she has ruled for the government in 92 percent of criminal cases; she has denied race claims in 83 percent of cases.... She has split evenly in a variety of employment cases.[15]

Schumer was right. In her eleven-year career on the Second Circuit Court of Appeals, Sotomayor had participated in nearly one hundred decisions involving race-based complaints and had sided against them in all but four of those cases. In one case, *Pappas v. Giuliani* (2002), which was decided by the Second Circuit in a 2–1 ruling, Sotomayor dissented from the majority ruling in favor of a white police officer who had mailed racist and anti-Semitic materials to groups that had solicited charitable donations from him. In this case, Nassau County, New York, police officer Thomas Pappas mailed back charitable contribution envelopes sent by the Mineola Auxiliary Police Department with flyers conveying anti-Black and anti-Semitic messages. Pappas, a member of the white nationalist National Association for the Advancement of White People, warned that "Negroes" were "destroying American civilization with rape, robbery, and murder," and that Jewish "control of TV networks" should be ceded to real Americans.[16] During her time on the Second Circuit, Sotomayor also participated in two panels that rejected rulings agreeing with race-based jury-selection claims. Though Schumer steered clear of these particular instances in which Sotomayor went far right of center on race-based claims, he nonetheless stated the obvious: the preponderance of evidence ironically demonstrated that Sotomayor had made rulings more aligned with conservative justices than either liberals or conservatives would have liked to believe.

The unrelenting focus on the "wise Latina" speech led to another instance of "proof" of Sotomayor's liberal activism. Commentators and pundits also focused on her alleged judicial activism in a case temporally close to her nomination. In *Ricci v. DeStefano* (2009) the plaintiff, Frank Ricci, a white firefighter from New Haven, Connecticut, alleged that he was discriminated against because of his race. Ricci claimed that he had passed a promotion test but that it was discarded when the test was deemed to demonstrate "disparate impact." The city of New Haven had discarded the test for everyone who took it. Ricci sued, and the case landed on the Second Circuit, where Sotomayor upheld the decision as consistent with existing law. According to Title VII directives, such tests are to be scrutinized to assess whether any racial disparities can be justified. Despite the overwhelming evidence found in her judicial record that Sotomayor's decisions had a decidedly conservative bias, the *Ricci* case helped solidify the wise Latina mediapheme's claim that she was a reverse racist.

Attacks on Sotomayor also came from left-of-center liberals. In a leaked memo to Obama, Harvard law professor Lawrence Tribe stated that "Sotomayor is not nearly as smart as she seems to think she is." Tribe's sexist invective against Sotomayor was even charitably read by some commentators less as a concern for her intellect than as a recognition that she simply was just not liberal enough. The confusion among Sotomayor the Nuyorican, Latinos writ large, and the false but tantalizing stories that the likes of Andy Martin promised, as well as the uncritical embrace of Sotomayor as the American dream incarnate, ultimately made her record subservient to the versions of the personal narratives that circulated as the "truth" about what became "the wise Latina" to some, "the lesbian cougar" to others, and the coordinates between these extremes. What is certain from all the versions of Sotomayor's life story that have since emerged is that Sotomayor signaled the arrival of Latino identity as an inescapable given in American political life; it also signaled the concomitant inability of national narratives to explain how Latinos do not simply come as immigrants or migrants to the United States but rather that "the United States [comes] to them in the form of colonial enterprises."[17]

It is clear that the Sotomayor mediapheme, along with the various iterations of white grievance resulting from claims of "reverse discrimination" after Sotomayor's nomination, required an architecture to make such historically untenable claims meaningful in the public sphere to a largely misinformed if not altogether uneducated citizenry. It is with some irony that the false narratives about Sotomayor that emerged during her confirmation hearings supplanted her judicial record and the evidence of her jurisprudential thinking. The facts weren't suppressed or kept from the Senate; rather, the alternative facts that emerged served to structure her confirmation hearings. The "wise Latina" mediapheme became the organizing attack based on unfounded assertions of "reverse racism" that would make whites the unjust victims of Latina injustice. Contrasted with the 2018 Senate confirmation hearings for Kavanaugh, for example, his full judicial record could be neither vetted nor reviewed. What is more, the allegations of sexual assault made against him by Dr. Christine Blasey Ford would not be fully explored by an FBI probe because the investigation was circumscribed by the

Trump White House. Whereas the "wise Latina" mediapheme relied on manufactured alt-facts for traction, the Kavanaugh confirmation hearings made white male heterosexual racial victimhood the defining mediapheme through which to understand the "truth" of the matter. The Constitution, a foundational document that Supreme Court justices are entrusted to uphold, was created by white male slave owners. That the Kavanaugh mediapheme posited white-male entitlement as an unprotected category under assault should condition our understanding of the limits of representative personhood in alt-right times.

The Kavanaugh mediapheme did borrow from the Sotomayor confirmation and named the mechanics involved a "smear campaign," except that the Sotomayor mediapheme, beyond being untrue, didn't have the scaffolding in the mediasphere to congeal. The so-called smear campaign had the support of senators and the president himself, who perpetuated the charge across media platforms. In the now infamous screed against those in the Senate Judiciary Committee who opposed his confirmation, Kavanaugh, in a spittle-inflected meltdown replete with shouting and acrimonious sarcasm, managed to attack the legislative branch (the Senate), with the support of the executive branch (the president), all the while vying for a seat on the judicial branch of government (the Supreme Court). He claimed that attempts to prevent his confirmation were part of a conspiracy and "revenge on behalf of the Clintons" for his previous work with Ken Starr to impeach former President Bill Clinton. This was significant. As with conspiracy theories, paranoid comportment and deportment are the outward manifestations of a "conviction that a secret, omnipotent individual or group covertly controls the political and social order."[18] It is with considerable irony that in spitting his defiance, Kavanaugh stated on the

Senate floor that he believed his own government was conspiring against him:

> Since my nomination in July, there's been a frenzy on the left to come up with something, anything to block my confirmation. Shortly after I was nominated, the Democratic Senate leader [Chuck Schumer, D-NY] said he would, quote, "oppose me with everything he's got." A Democratic senator [Cory Booker, D-NJ] on this committee publicly—publicly referred to me as evil—evil. Think about that word. It's said that those who supported me were, quote, "complicit in evil." Another Democratic senator on this committee [Richard Blumenthal, D-CT] said, quote, "Judge Kavanaugh is your worst nightmare." A former head of the Democratic National Committee [Wendy Wasserman Schultz] said, quote, "Judge Kavanaugh will threaten the lives of millions of Americans for decades to come" [former Virginia governor Terry McAuliffe (D) had also said this]....
> I would say to those senators, your words have meaning. Millions of Americans listen carefully to you. Given comments like those, is it any surprise that people have been willing to do anything to make any physical threat against my family, to send any violent e-mail to my wife, to make any kind of allegation against me and against my friends.... You sowed the wind for decades to come. I fear that the whole country will reap the whirlwind.[19]

The accusations Kavanaugh levied against Senate Democrats and liberals alike were aped by North Carolina GOP senator Lindsey Graham in his own screed in support of Kavanaugh during the hearings. Graham, who had famously noted during Sotomayor's own confirmation hearing that she would likely get confirmed as long she didn't have a "meltdown," appeared unconcerned about his or Kavanaugh's outburst. That it was Graham himself and Kavanaugh who had meltdowns during the proceedings should lay to rest any doubts about the double standard that inheres when ethnic gendered subjects such as

Sotomayor are held to considerably higher standards than shouting, aggrieved, angry white men.

After Kavanaugh's confirmation, Trump expanded the "smear campaign" mediapheme further until it congealed in its most toxic form. Trump called the allegations against Kavanaugh a "complete and utter hoax." After the confirmation, Trump told reporters at the White House that Democrats had orchestrated the hoax. Attacking the opposition party, along with news outlets, such as CNN, that the president considers unfavorable to him, he said, "It was all made up—it was fabricated, and it's a disgrace." That the president was lying was inconsequential to the mediapheme's incarnation *as* a hoax: it reasserted the president's own strategy of denial in the face of at least fourteen allegations of sexual assault and sexual impropriety levied against him. Additionally, by calling Dr. Ford's allegations a hoax, the Trump mediapheme became not just a weapon with which to wage a national assault on abuse survivors, but a means of funneling alt-right furor in an effort to influence the November 2018 midterm elections by characterizing anyone against the administration's prerogatives as a "mob." Trump's narrative framing of democratic dissent as "mob rule" further solidified his previous Department of Justice directives to introduce legislation banning protests in retribution against his administration's war on civil liberties.[20] Shortly after Kavanaugh's confirmation, the president announced that he considered himself a proud "nationalist." The "nationalist" dog whistle telegraphed support for white nationalists, the radical right, and those clustered around the president's *Breitbart News* base. (*Breitbart News* is a far-right, white nationalist "news" organization. Trump appointed *Breitbart News* executive chairman Steve Bannon as his chief strategist after his election in 2016 and served with him at the White

House until August 2017.) That Kavanaugh was confirmed should alarm us for what it means for the judiciary, the country, and the futures of the democratic commons. Would such a meltdown have allowed Sotomayor to survive as a viable candidate to the Supreme Court during her confirmation hearings? How could Kavanaugh have been confirmed after credible allegations emerged of sexual assault, binge drinking, and perjury? What's more, what architecture could possibly sustain the "Clinton conspiracy theory" that Kavanaugh alleged in front of millions of viewers during the hearings? Understanding how this came to be is crucial to understanding both the afterlife of democratic practice as well as its futures in our posttruth, postfacts, conspiracy theory–driven historical moment.

This is especially significant when we consider the attempted mail pipe bomb attacks of October 24, 2018, against Obama, the Clintons, former attorney general Eric Holder, former Democratic National Committee director and Florida congressperson Debbie Wasserman Schultz, New Jersey Democratic senator and Senate Judiciary Committee member Cory Booker, and New York governor Andrew Cuomo, as well as CNN headquarters in New York and other individuals and entities associated with the Democratic Party.[21] Kavanaugh's prediction that the country would "reap the whirlwind" came true in short order. Yet the alleged antidemocratic reactionaries Kavanaugh denigrated in his conspiracy-laden screed weren't the liberal scapegoats he accused of inciting violence against him and his family but rather the emboldened alt-right nationalists who saw fit to attack the opposition as the enemy of the people. Kavanaugh's screed worked like an incantation that awakened the fearmongering the president had used relentlessly: the liberal press is "the enemy of the people." Kavanaugh's incantation, "I fear that the whole country will reap the whirlwind," fed the metaphorical flame and literally carried it in the mail to the doorsteps of enemies he and the president had identified. It would not be an exaggeration to contend that Kavanaugh's attack provided a blueprint for attacking both those described as "liberal hoaxters" by the president and those entrusted to check presidential authority. The pipe bombs were sent to several "liberals" on Kavanaugh's list, including Booker and Wasserman Schultz, whose Florida office address was included as the return address on all the bomb packages. Simply put, Kavanaugh's screed before the Senate Judiciary Committee served as a blueprint for the military-like attack on the opposition that enveloped the nation on October 24, 2018.

The president exacerbated the situation in characteristic fashion. The day after the majority of the bombs were sent to several figures identified in Kavanaugh's screed, the president himself kept a scheduled political pep rally in Wisconsin. At the rally, as the nation reeled from the terrorist attacks, Trump fans shouted their signature attack on Hillary Clinton, "Lock her up!" It was of no consequence to either the president or the audience that one of the bombs was addressed to Hillary Clinton. In his teleprompted speech, Trump said the country needed to come together in "peace and harmony," yet he attacked the media in the very same speech. "The media also has a responsibility to set a civil tone and to stop the endless hostility and constant negative and oftentimes false attacks and stories," he said in a not so veiled attack on CNN, whose offices had been evacuated after receiving one of the pipe bombs the day before. Those who must abide by "civility," he seemed to say, were those who disagreed with his politics or those who needed to be disciplined for reporting facts about his politics that were buttressed by evidence. Which is to say that anyone demanding respect for the rule of

law, and the necessary checks and balances required of democratic governance, needed to be "civilized" into submission.
These calls for "civility" under the Trump regime have become
a form of alt-right "political correctness" that refuses to distinguish between the berating of a politician in public for caging
children at the border and an outright terrorist attack against
Trump's political opposition. When the president suggested that
week in a tweet that the bomb scares were a ruse to dissuade
Republican voters from voting in the November elections, it was
clear that any pretense or regard for proper governance was a
thing of the past. The goal was simply unadulterated agitprop in
the service of suppressing any form of opposition to Trumpism.
The nation had crossed a line. Trump ushered the country into
the realm of dictatorial regimes seeped in the fascist and separa-
tist tactics of the last century: exalting the supremacy of a white
nation while discrediting the state's institutional apparatus for
the necessary checks and balances on absolutist power. But the
events that culminated in the October 2018 attacks against those
considered enemies of the president had been ideologically
scaffolded decades before. The foundation for the ethnoracial
separatism that exalted the nation over the state had already
largely been engineered by none other than Newt Gingrich and
the representatives ushered into Congress with the so-called
Republican Revolution of 1994. If that seems like an exaggeration, let us proceed to the facts at hand.

DEMOCRACY'S AFTERLIFE AND THE END
OF EXPERTISE IN THE COMMONS

It is admittedly difficult to imagine that erstwhile presidential
hopeful and former House conservative leader Newt Gingrich

would pose significant threats to democratic thinking or the architecture of checks and balances that sustains democratic practice. If there were ever a poster boy for hot-air political braggadocio in the national imaginary, it would likely be Gingrich. Gingrich, unlike second- or third-tier political pundits like Sean Hannity or Rush Limbaugh, has understood American political culture in ways sobering and calculating enough to require us to pause and consider how and why his rise to power in the early 1990s matters deeply to our posttruth, "alternative facts" moment, which culminated with Trump's presidency and its violent aftermath.

Investigative journalists Paul Glastris and Haley Sweetland Edwards have made the case that Gingrich, while he was speaker of the House from 1995 to 1999, became one of the primary architects of the collapse of checks and balances. In their significant exposé, "The Big Lobotomy," Glastris and Sweetland Edwards explain how Gingrich effectively stripped "Congress of the intellectual capacity it needed to function as a co-equal branch of government" and did so, most significantly, when he effectively "laid off a third of the 'professional staff' who advised Members of Congress and provided much of the legislature's institutional expertise."[22] The gutting of expertise and fact-checking began with the elimination of professional researchers and investigators, who removed misinformation from governmental reporting and managed data in the service of gathering facts that would inform policy. The ability to distinguish truth from fiction was a primary casualty as governmental expertise diminished by moving much of the high-level decisions on legislation from the committees that relied on professional researchers to the party leaders' offices.

As noted by Glastris and Sweetland Edwards, after Gingrich's rise to power the Congressional Research Service (CRS)—

which has functioned as the research arm of Congress—suffered considerable losses in support staff, which was composed of degreed professional researchers. Astoundingly, the CRS began to recruit more student interns from lawmakers' home states to make up for the "brain drain."[23] It is during this signal moment that we can trace the genesis of our current epistemic impasse, in which "alternative facts" and falsehoods are supported by the president and perpetuated by the reigning political regime through its media conglomerates. The evisceration of congressional expertise was certainly something without parallel in American history and Gingrich's "Contract with America" (1994) helped enshrine the rise of the winner-takes-all politics we have inherited today in addition to the gutting of expertise described by Glastris and Sweetland Edwards.

The Contract with America was a Republican Party platform document created by Gingrich, and other neocon leaders, that helped Republicans get elected and become the majority in the U.S. House of Representatives for the first time in forty years after the 1994 congressional election. The Contract outlined a neoconservative blueprint and action plan based on economic and "conservative social values" that had been espoused by the neocon Heritage Foundation since the 1970s. Gingrich himself noted the importance of the Contract shortly after getting elected in early 1995, though admittedly for grandiose reasons impervious to the looming damage to American institutions, when he described it as a historical and foundational text. He said there simply existed "no comparable congressional document in our two-hundred-year history."[24] That Gingrich effectively eliminated what the country needed to make informed policy decisions possible appears to have been of no consequence to him. His first move was to quickly slash the budgets and staff of the House committees, thereby evacuating the expertise and historical memory associated with the CRS. The decline of expertise resulted in arguably some of the worst political decisions of our time, including the invasion of Iraq (based on false claims of weapons of mass destruction), which destabilized the region and the world; "controversy" over climate change science; financial (de)regulation; racialized carceral policies; and the arrival of alternative facts befitting a totalitarian regime. Bruce Bartlett, conservative economist and top economic adviser for both Ronald Reagan (1911–14) and George H. W. Bush (1924–2018), noted that Gingrich "always considered himself to be the smartest guy in the room and long chafed at being corrected by experts when he cooked up some new plan, over which he may have expended 30 seconds of thought, to completely upend and remake the health, tax or education systems."[25] For Bartlett, Gingrich did "everything in his power to dismantle Congressional institutions that employed people with the knowledge, training and experience to know a harebrained idea when they saw it." It is a question of consequence that today the same could be said of Trump.

Gingrich, along with Representative Dick Armey (R-TX) and the other GOP neocons, introduced these structural transformations into the fiber of American civic and judicial life through the Contract.[26] The Contract itself served as both the structural architecture and vision platform of the GOP in order to gain greater control over tax legislation, push corporate deregulation, and make massive cuts to public education spending, which have led to historic levels of student indebtedness. As noted, the ultraconservative Heritage Foundation's economic and "social reform" served as the basis for the Contract and one of its principal goals was to diminish government spending on social programs while expanding tort reform through deregulation in the service of corporations. The results were astounding and significant both in their reach and the rhetorical expediency through which draconian measures were couched in the language of palliative reform for an infirm body politic.

The Contract with America created by the 104th Congress ultimately led to a two-pronged battle that sought both social and economic "reforms." The social battle attempted to contain and control minority populations, while its concomitant economic battle sought to provide the necessary deregulation that ushered in the vast accumulation of wealth we have today in the hands of the proverbial "one percenters." This was accomplished by legally strengthening the neoliberal economic order's three pillars under the guise of benevolent reforms. The three principal neoliberal pillars of austerity—privatization, economic efficiency, and personal responsibility—permeated the domains of the social and the economic to the detriment of minority communities, as well as wage earners, irrespective of class, ethnic, or racial affiliation. The subtending fictions of the Contract were premised on racist assumptions about minorities and the poor. The Contract understood "economic efficiency" in absolutist terms that included massive cuts to public welfare spending and the need for a "balanced budget" above the needs of economically ravaged communities; "privatization" as a corrective to government spending for the public good in sectors such as education and welfare (but not in defense spending); and "personal responsibility" in terms of controlling the lives and reproductive choices of communities of color. It is an often overlooked fact that after the implementation of the Contract, Gingrich made headlines after recommending that children be taken from "unfit" parents and placed in orphanages. While that recommendation didn't appear in the Contract's final iteration, it is seen today in Trump senior adviser Steven Miller's border plan resulting in the separation of migrant children at the border. Many of these have been placed in orphanages with links to the family of Trump's education secretary, Betsy DeVos.[27] (As of this writing, Bethany Christian Services, founded by the family of DeVos, has received at least eighty-one children taken from their parents at the U.S. border.[28]) Indeed, the Contract enshrined in the public and private sectors the organizational logics and structures of neoliberal austerity and cruelty, which have come to define our moment. Though there were two battlefronts, it was the social battle that hit and punished communities of color the hardest.

Representative examples of the many bills that the Contract with America produced that disproportionately affected communities of color and, it must be said, queers, included the following: the Taking Back Our Streets Act, which sought to criminalize minor offenses, extend the death penalty for petty crimes, and establish related "zero-tolerance" measures that have resulted in the mass incarceration of Black and Brown bodies; the Personal Responsibility Act, which sought to discourage the birth of "illegitimate children" and teen pregnancy by prohibiting public assistance to teen mothers and denying any additional public assistance to "welfare queens" who had additional children;[29] the American Dream Restoration Act, which sought to use tax benefits to encourage married, high-income heterosexuals to have more children, which, given the correlation of race and income in the United States, would mean more white children; the National Security Restoration Act, which sought to prevent U.S. troops from serving under United Nations command and laid the groundwork for the United States' refusal to abide by UN decrees and the eventual U.S. departure in 2018 from the UN Human Rights Council because it was a "cesspool for political bias";[30] the Common Sense Legal Reform Act, which sought to reduce "frivolous" litigation for the benefit of corporations and government interests, resulting in contamination in predominantly minority communities from Flint, Michigan, to Puerto Rico and beyond; and the Family Reinforcement Act, which, among other things, exerted greater control over what constitutes "lewd" or "obscene" media. Most importantly, the Family Reinforcement Act sought to provide tax incentives for heterosexual couples to adopt children and give parents "freedom of choice," allowing them to use public tax dollars for private, religiously affiliated schools if they didn't want their children to attend public schools. This, it must be emphatically noted, has irreparably broken the only American wall worth building: the Jeffersonian wall between church and state, which has now ruptured and allowed "Christian bakers" the right to deny equal service to LGBTQ communities.

This turn toward neoconservative activism on the Supreme Court was initiated in tandem with the work of the Heritage Foundation through the founding of the Federalist Society for Law and Public Policy Studies at Harvard, Yale, and the University of Chicago in 1982. In 1981, during Reagan's first presidency, his calls for "judicial restraint" rhetorically hid the striking level of neocon judicial activism that was set to take place through his Department of Justice. Reagan's strategy was simple: create an army of neoconservative ideologues who would inject conservative ideology into the national judiciary. Reagan effectively "sought to groom a cadre of well-credentialed conservative lawyers and, in so doing, transform constitutional discourse and judicial decision-making."[31] That very cadre of legal minds seeped in doctrinaire textualist or originalist interpretations of the law is now in all corners of the judiciary and legislative branches of government, as well as the nation's law schools. The Supreme Court's Federalist Society ideologues now dominate the court: John G. Roberts, Clarence Thomas, Samuel Alito, Neil Gorsuch, and Brett Kavanaugh control the most ideologically engineered Supreme Court in the history of its existence.

Equally significant, we would do well to brace for the consequences of Trump's other judicial appointments. Trump has made a record forty-one appointments to U.S. District Courts and has had twenty-six Court of Appeals judges confirmed; they now occupy slightly over 15 percent of the nation's circuit judgeships. And that percentage is increasing precipitously in comparison to all previous presidencies.[32] The Heritage Foundation, along with the Federalist Society and other ultraconservative groups, like the Judicial Crisis Network and the Judicial Action Group, have for years sought to develop a new generation of younger legal conservatives who would go into government and fill the lower levels of the judiciary and, as they have done, transform the Supreme Court into the bastion of conservative legal bias that it is. And they have succeeded. During the Kavanaugh confirmation vote, Senator Dick Durbin (D-IL) and other senators noted the obvious: for the first time in the country's history the White House had outsourced the work of vetting candidates for the Supreme Court to the ultraconservative Federalist Society and the Heritage Foundation. The scaffolding for conservative judicial activism that began after the founding of the Federalist Society was sedimented in the Contract with America, which made jurisprudence and neocon lawyering central to its programmatic goals. While early civil rights lawyers like Thurgood Marshall had sought decades earlier to ensure equal rights and protections for all Americans, the

Contract's legislative ideologues made destroying these early civil rights gains their principal goal in the guise of a judicial philosophy of "universality" that is out of touch with the history of equality of opportunity for all Americans. It is not an exaggeration to concede that well after Trump leaves office, the courts will have been fully radicalized by the alt-right to the diminishment of civil liberties for all Americans.

The results of the Contract were as swift as they were stunning. After the first one hundred days alone, the majority-Republican 104th Congress had done away with the checks and balances that allowed for the evaluation of evidence to inform and direct policy in all facets of governance and public policy. No less consequential, the newly emerging internet and web-based news outlets began to create the perfect historical confluence of events for the disavowal of "evidence" in public and private life through the à la carte selection of "facts" through confirmation bias. (In sociological research *confirmation bias* describes the practice of embracing information that conforms to one's worldview while simultaneously ignoring and rejecting information or facts that contradict one's prejudices.) That the decline in public education funding dropped precipitously in the 1990s just as the rise of "alternative news" outlets began to proliferate should inform our understanding of the crisis at hand. Indeed, understanding the education crisis in our present requires proper framing for an understanding of the Latino question after Trumpism.

Having gutted government expertise for policy, the Contract with America's austerity measures also had a direct impact on the county's higher education landscape. In 1992, for example, a mere three years before the 104th Congress enacted its Contract with America, tuition accounted for slightly less than three-tenths of the total educational revenue for public colleges and universities. Today, public colleges and universities can no longer rely on state appropriations to support educating the population. The funding decline in state appropriations for colleges and universities has made tuition higher than ever, reduced the quality of educational delivery, and forced institutions to balance their budgets by reducing faculty, eviscerating library resources, limiting course offerings, and in some cases closing campuses. Today, "at a time when the benefit of a college education has never been greater, state policymakers have made going to college less affordable and less accessible to the students most in need."[33] This means that tuition at public institutions is higher than ever precisely when it is needed the most in order to provide economic opportunity and social mobility. Tuition now accounts for nearly a third of the operating revenue for public higher education institutions in the United States.

The seismic proportions of this impasse represent a "historic shift away from tax dollars funding the bulk of public higher education" for the public good.[34] And that seismic shift had profound implications for communities of color and the poor. For education journalist Ronald Brownstein, this recalibration of the purpose of higher education spending in the country came

> precisely as the nation's youth population [was] crossing a succession of milestones to become more racially diverse than ever. As statisticians would say, it's an open question whether these twin trends represent an example of causation or just correlation. But whether resources are shrinking because diversity is growing, or the two trends are proceeding independently, their convergence is still a dangerous development—not only for higher education, but also for the nation's economic future.[35]

Even if seen solely in instrumentalist terms, the higher education crisis is significant because it puts the nation at an economic disadvantage. While Brownstein leaves the correlational inference between social stratification and education up to his readers, other studies are unambiguous about how the nation is losing the gains made through educational access policies such as affirmative action.

Today, for example, while proportionally more Latinos are attending colleges and universities, the increase has not kept up with the growth of the Latino college-age population in the United States, so the gap between students and the college-age Latino population has in fact widened rather than diminished. The same is true for Blacks. "Black students today make up 9 percent of the freshmen at Ivy League schools but 15 percent of college-age Americans, roughly the same gap as in 1980."[36] Traditionally underrepresented students remain as underrepresented today in higher education as they did in the 1980s. What's more, the Contract's austerity measures, coupled with its muscular social agenda to contain Black and Brown bodies, did away with the gains that made higher education accessible to the likes of Sotomayor and Obama. While Gingrich called Obama the first food stamp president, and Sotomayor an undeserving "Latina racist," the scaffolding he largely helped to build through the Contract ensured that such possibilities for Black and Brown mobility would be further diminished, if not altogether eliminated, for generations to come. It is in this context that we must understand Sotomayor, whose story of social mobility is today a foreclosed possibility for the scores of Black and Brown bodies that want a seat at the table. As we saw in chapter 2, the death of affirmative action after the *Bakke* case was the first deathblow to Black and Brown social mobility through education. The Contract with America, its legacies and policies, have largely created the scaffolding that makes "representative characters" such as Obama and Sotomayor the exceptions that prove the rule of national exclusion.

With the daunting demographic changes occasioned by the Latino majority minority, it is not inconsequential that Latino educational attainment is being stymied at every turn. The creation of a permanent underclass requires limiting educational attainment, controlling physical and social mobility, and questioning the very humanity of Latinos. If Latino children are still in cages as of this writing, and they are, one must acknowledge that delimiting the spaces that Latino bodies may access has been a central preoccupation of the social engineers of the Contract with America and its subtending fictions about Black and Brown "genetic" inferiority. The dehumanization of the Latino body goes hand in hand with the "Build that wall!" xenophobia that allows the likes of Trump to conflate Mexicans with all people of Latin American ancestry in the United States. Not surprisingly, immigration "reform" as a type of social containment is central to the attack on Latinos writ large.

Jason Richwine, the right-wing neocon discussed in chapter 1, who resigned from the Heritage Foundation amid controversy surrounding his "research" linking Latino genetic inferiority to low levels of Latino educational achievement, helped Trump craft his immigration policies as well as the "Muslim ban." Shortly after leaving the Heritage Foundation, he joined the Center for Immigration Studies (CIS). The CIS, a relatively new Washington, DC, neocon advocacy organization and think tank that emerged early in the 2016 presidential campaign, has consistently provided talking points that Trump repeatedly uses in his anti-Latino assaults on Twitter and in related media outlets. Richwine has continually asserted that the "new Hispanic immigrants will have low-IQ children and grandchildren." After the 2016 election, Richwine said,

> I'm honestly delighted that Trump is putting a team together that has such reasonable views on immigration. This was almost impossible to imagine even just a year ago.... It's clear that Trump has opened up space to talk about immigration in a way we haven't been able to before.[37]

The space that Trumpism has opened up for alternative facts and the ensuing slow death of democratic practice, not to mention the ability to distinguish truth from alt-right fictions, would have indeed been impossible to imagine were it not for the blueprint enshrined in the so-called Contact with America, which the Heritage Foundation helped to craft and disseminate. The same could be said about the rise of Kavanaugh and his eventual confirmation to the Supreme Court. While the corrective challenges at hand are many, understanding the stakes from the vantage point of those with the most to lose is now indistinguishable from the exigencies of the Latino question. What can Latino practices of freedom teach America about fortifying democratic practice?

Beyond the Sotomayor mediapheme, and the space for craven opportunism created by misinformation through the gutting of expertise, understanding the Latino question allows us to understand the costs, responsibilities, and the limits associated with a seat at the national table. We must endeavor to reclaim, protect, and fortify the boisterous, messy space of the democratic commons. Sonia Sotomayor is a formidable test case in this regard. How might her own transformation as an associate justice, in a climate of unimaginable racism steeped in the denigration of Latino life and the waning of democratic practice, inspire new political actors to emerge? What lessons can we glean from the trajectory of Sotomayor, the country's best-known Latino figure, and her indebtedness to the American dream, which ostensibly led her to the Supreme Court? So it is to the futures of the Latino question and the state of Latino debt that I now turn.

CHAPTER FOUR

Sonia Sotomayor and Other States of Debt

> The progression of my life has been uniquely
> American. My parents left Puerto Rico during World
> War II.... My father, a factory worker with a third-
> grade education, passed away when I was 9 years old.
> On her own, my mother raised my brother and me.
> She taught us that the key to success in America is a
> good education. And she set the example, studying
> alongside my brother and me at our kitchen table
> so she could become a registered nurse. We worked
> hard.
>
> Sonia Sotomayor[1]

Sotomayor's entry into American civic life was a story about debt.
When she was finally confirmed by the Senate Judiciary Committee (SJQ), she held the dubious honor of being the most indebted
sitting justice on the court. The parallels between her own debts
and Puerto Rico's were striking. Puerto Rico is the most indebted
sociopolitical space under U.S. jurisdiction, and Supreme Court
associate justice Sotomayor, the Bronx-born daughter of Puerto
Rican migrants, was the most indebted justice in the history of
the court. Sotomayor's financial records included in her SJQ ques-

tionnaire noted that she was over $30,000 in debt, including medical bills not covered by her insurance plan. Though modest by upper-middle-class standards, her debt was touted as evidence of her "lack of restraint," her "gaudy taste in clothes and 'yellow-gold' earrings," and even her "unnaturally white looking teeth [that] she [was] still paying for." In short, debt was cast as both an unrestrained aesthetic practice with disastrous financial consequences and as ontological "evidence" of her "ethnic excesses," all despite her lack of capital. What the SJQ report could not empirically quantify was the broader indebtedness that had inhered in the narrative of upward mobility created by her and the Obama administration. Her debt was narrativized as a story of "immigrant" indebtedness to the nation. Sotomayor was indebted to affirmative action, though it had been effectively neutralized at the time of her appointment; she was indebted to her "hardworking single mother who gave up her dreams so Sonia [Sotomayor] could pursue the 'American Dream'"; she was indebted to her "ethic of hard work beyond the poverty and crime that characterized her upbringing in a Bronx tenement"; and she was indebted, of course, to the first African American president. Indeed, her incorporation into the U.S. body politic, her indebtedness to the greater largesse of U.S. institutions, made her an assimilable subject that other Latinos and undoubtedly other indebted Americans could ostensibly emulate.

It is with some irony that the president who nominated Sotomayor was also the one who signed the Puerto Rico Oversight, Management, and Economic Stability Act in 2016. The act, known as PROMESA, created the Fiscal Control Board (FCB), composed of unelected overseers whose principal purpose is to protect financial investors. The FCB constituted the recognition that a fiscal "state of emergency" superseded the needs of Puerto Ricans and their institutions for the sake of restructuring debt, all for the benefit of creditors. PROMESA enabled the island's government to enter a bankruptcy-like restructuring and halt all litigation related to the island's actual or potential future loan defaults. That Sotomayor became intelligible and visible as a colonial subject who was assimilable within the American body politic through a corollary logic of debt and indebtedness ultimately elided the historical accounting that would make her arrival to the bench all the more spectacular. This chapter situates and critiques how Sotomayor's various states of indebtedness paradoxically allowed for the erasure of a broader historical debt: the degree to which U.S. national wealth on the island and elsewhere has been premised on colonial "capital extraction" campaigns.[2] In international legal theory, debts are considered illegitimate and described as "odious" if they are incurred by a regime that does not serve the nation. In this chapter, I explore the implications of odious debt in the making of Puerto Rico and its ancillary logics in the making of Sotomayor as a representative Latina.

Sotomayor's telling of her own life story, of course, *necessarily* had to read like a page from the national multicultural storybook of inclusion made possible by the American dream narrative. As we saw in previous chapters, the American dream is far from a category devoid of analytical use value; ultimately, it exalts a particular form of nationalism that disengages cause-effect historical relations by subordinating the cost of U.S. empire building in the Caribbean, and elsewhere, to cultural narratives of inclusion for postcolonial national subjects. Indeed, even at its best, the effect of this most recent iteration of the American dream *as* debt is the erasure of empire's historical specificity and its illegitimate appropriation of property, power, and human capital. Sotomayor's tale of sacrifice and her parents' *immigration*—never described during her nomination as *colonial migration* from Puerto Rico—was presented alongside anecdotes of how study, determination, and diligence served as the necessary antidotes to overcoming poverty, language barriers, and discrimination in an America where social mobility was possible through education and the sheer will to succeed. Sotomayor herself couched her story and her parents' as one of labor and indebtedness. As noted previously, "My mother raised my brother and me [and] taught us that the key to success in America is a good education.... We worked hard." It is undoubtedly a valuable story, one she expanded considerably in her enormously successful *New York Times* best-selling memoir, *My Beloved World* (2013), which—not coincidentally—got her out of debt. I am here interested in reading her family's story of migration in relation to U.S.–Puerto Rican colonial history, which has been almost completely evacuated from discussions surrounding her representative "Latinaness." In the process, I hope to show how the limits of Latino national incorporation, and the conditions under which inclusion and political enfranchisement can be either granted or denied to Latino subjects, requires deep historical accounting. Indeed, had anyone bothered to look beyond the Sotomayor mediapheme I discussed in chapter 3— the narrative moving target outside history proper—they would have actually learned a great deal about the price of the seat at the table. And it is to that lost opportunity that I now turn.

POSTCOLONIAL DEBTS

Central to the multicultural liberal democratic narrative that subtends Sotomayor's life story is a notion of representative personhood that claims to stand for the greatest social good. As we have seen, it is a narrative that ultimately triumphed when Sotomayor was confirmed with a *Brown* twist. Obama, the president of hope, translated his rebranding of the American dream to a new generation of voters, and *Brown* voters to be, through a narrative structure steeped in a mythology of identification and assimilation for the nation's largest minority. Sotomayor, identifiably Latina and incorporated into the national fold through the confirmation process, enacted a relation to the state that made the belief in assimilation plausible to the nation's largest minority— Latinos as the nation's "sleeping giant," in the language of electoral politics—and, potentially, the country's largest voting bloc.

"In all people, I see myself," wrote the great poet of democracy in the paean to democratic equality "Song of Myself," from his *Leaves of Grass* (1855). Walt Whitman remains America's great poet-evangelist of democratic hope for a better union and Obama the most recent but failed translator of hope, as the waves of post-Obama alt-right white nationalists have made clear. Still, "Song of Myself," as the national hymn to the promise of democratic inclusion, was reinterpreted and made intelligible long enough for its newest Latina representative character to gain a seat at the table. It is in this sense that Sotomayor becomes a figure through whom the "slumbering" political subjects' values, aspirations, and achievements can be made intelligible to both the majority culture and the country's Latino majority minority. For this narrative to be intelligible in the public sphere, Sotomayor's story necessarily had to begin in medias res, in the middle of a national story dependent on stock characters and exhausted tropes. Yet the narrative instantiation of a life in medias res—a life worth telling only when she becomes "American" through the values she assumes as her own—both comes at a cost to its literal referent, Sotomayor, and assumes the form of the most recent and disastrous post-Obama American dream. And what can such a national pedagogy premised on assimilation through identification teach us beyond the stereotypes it asks us to assume? If the moral of Sotomayor's life story is one of success through hard work and education, then "hope" is the enabling fiction that regenerates the American dream of mobility and social inclusion in our current moment of historical crisis. But such a dream of inclusion requires the nation's slumbering subjects to sleepwalk through history. Because Sotomayor is a child of colonial subjects whose migration to New York was occasioned by the U.S. occupation of Puerto Rico, her narrative of inclusion evinces a predilection for historical amnesia as the precondition for ethnic subjects to enter American civic life; real democratic practice requires, however, that we demand an accounting of this. So let us then turn to the colonial detritus of empire's remains.

EMPIRE'S REMAINS

As Sotomayor often remarks in graduation addresses and speeches, "The more interesting part of my life is really the story of my mother's life." Curiously, though we know very little about Celina Báez's life, especially her girlhood years in Puerto Rico, we still know more about her private life than we do about her daughter's. The deflection about Sotomayor's personal life, though certainly not coincidental given the versions circulated by the mediapheme, also allows her own desexualized womanhood to be understood as both the cost (the sacrifice) and the dividends (the payoff) associated with *being* Latina as a state of virtuous deference to the mother. Against the infamous 1980s "welfare queen," who, according to President Reagan, "turned the social safety net into a hammock," the figure of the virtuous mother lives for her children's future, not her own. Through example, she teaches that sacrifice and personal abnegation ultimately bear dividends: her children's cultural capital. The story of Celina Báez's sacrifice, real as it was by all accounts, also becomes part of the enabling fiction for Sotomayor's own success and seeming disavowal of her own affective life.

From interviews to press releases, Báez's life has been a story of triumph in the face of great odds. Whereas Sotomayor's father passed away when she was nine, Celina Báez's mother, bedridden with health problems for years, died when the she was nine as well. Shortly after, Báez's father promptly abandoned the family. Left parentless, Báez was raised by her older sister, Aurora, in San Germán, Puerto Rico, a farming village near Mayagüez, on the westernmost corner of the island. When she was seventeen, Celina Báez left the island on the heels of World War II after she was recruited for the war effort by the Women's Army Corps. Alone and not knowing a word of English, or how to answer a telephone, as Sotomayor has said of her mother's war years, Celina was sent to Fort Oglethorpe in northwest Georgia, were she learned "how to handle a gas mask," which included "trips into [a] gas chamber" to regulate effective breathing under stress (see author website, figure 4).[3] The fear of German biological warfare after the United States entered World War I had turned Puerto Rico into the United States' Gibraltar.

Puerto Rico would represent the first theater of war if the Axis powers attacked the United States. Already as early as 1917—before the United States officially entered the World War I on April 2, 1917—the passage of the Jones Act had ensured that Puerto Ricans were made U.S. citizens through an act of Congress that allowed their conscription into the U.S. armed forces (we would do well to remember that during every major conflict since World War I, Latino soldiers have been the first to die). When World War I ended, over 22,000 Puerto Rican soldiers had served in the U.S. armed forces after they were conscripted. In regiments such as the well-known Harlem Hellcats, and the lesser-known 65th Infantry Regiment of Puerto Rico, Puerto Rican soldiers who, like Celina Báez decades later, spoke no English at all, represented the first line of defense in the Great War. In fact, it was a Puerto Rican, Teófilo Marxuach, who is credited with firing the first shot for the United States, from El Morro fortress, when the German vessel *Odenwald* approached San Juan harbor. The psychological effects of not knowing the language when they were conscripted made Puerto Rican soldiers quite literally the first corporeal line of defense against enemy combatants.[4] By World War II, the military apparatus on the island had already developed a biological weapons protocol that was part of the Puerto Rican National Guard's basic training regimen. Báez's training in the Puerto Rican's Women Army Corps's (WAC) biological weapons program at Fort Oglethorpe emphasized how to care for the sick and how to triage patients while wearing a gas mask. In the first theater of war, the "Number 1 defensive outpost for the U.S. on the Atlantic," the training of the Puerto Rican WAC stressed preparation for returning to the island if needed "to care for the sick and wounded, and otherwise contaminated" population (*WAC Handbook*).[5] It is with some irony that in the year Báez left the island (1944), Puerto Rican Nationalists were decrying the use of political prisoners for radiological and virological experimentation by U.S. colonial authorities under various Rockefeller Foundation public health initiatives.

According to Pedro Albizu Campos (1891–1965), the Harvard-educated Nationalist Party leader and himself a former U.S.

Army lieutenant in World War I, Nationalist prisoners on the island had since 1932 been subjected to radiological experimentation under the direction of the Rockefeller Foundation's Dr. Cornelius Rhoads. Albizu Campos claimed that he himself had been subjected to radiation poisoning since his first incarceration under Rhoads's "care," and with the help of a sympathetic guard, his claim as well as an accompanying photograph of his irradiated body was reproduced in at least three Latin American newspapers. The press in Puerto Rico was prevented from covering this since the 1901 Supreme Court case *Downes v. Bidwell* determined that constitutional protections could not apply in Puerto Rico since it was an "unincorporated territory." Coterminous with the alleged biological and radiological experiments on the island, the U.S. Department of Health, Education and Welfare's involvement with one of the most underanalyzed chapters in the history of colonial biopower offers a telling frame of Báez's "immigration" to the United States.

BIOPOWER AND PUERTO RICO

Since the United States assumed governance of Puerto Rico in 1898 after the Spanish American War, population control became a major concern. Between the world wars, U.S. concern about overpopulation on the island led to public policies aimed at controlling the rapid growth of the population, or "biomanagement," the management of life on the island. The passage of Law 116 in 1937 institutionalized population control in Puerto Rico as U.S colonial policy.[6] The U.S. Department of Health, Education, and Welfare's Law 116 mandated a eugenicist sterilization program that had enduring and profound consequences on the island. This program, designed by the Eugenics Board under the supervision of Planned Parenthood founder Margaret Sanger (1879–1966), was intended to "catalyze economic growth" and respond to "Depression-era unemployment." Eugenicists in the United States, like Sanger, "seized on the resulting poverty, blaming overpopulation, and targeting poor women for sterilization and pharmaceutical experimentation" in Puerto Rico.[7] Both U.S. government funds and contributions from private individuals supported these initiatives on the island. Most striking, these initiatives led to the most extensive mass sterilization program in the world.

As Iris López reminds us in her groundbreaking book *Matters of Choice: Puerto Rican Women's Struggle for Reproductive Freedom,* from 1930 to 1970 approximately one-third of Puerto Rico's female population of childbearing age had undergone *la operación,* or "the operation," a euphemism for sterilization undertaken without patient consent.[8] So common was the practice that the words *sterilization* and *la operación* were used interchangeably. In her study, López documents and repeats what the Puerto Rican Nationalists had already shouted to deaf ears through clandestine pamphlets, illegal speeches, veiled press reporting, and even elite literary expression, including René Marqués's signature play, *Los soles truncos* (1958), which used exquisite symbology to avoid censors and censure after the consolidation of the Law of the Muzzle in 1948. Known popularly as *la ley de la mordaza,* colonial Law 53 made it illegal to stage dissent or opposition to U.S. colonial authority in Puerto Rico in the press or through any other means. For example, the law made it a crime to display a Puerto Rican flag, sing patriotic tunes, talk or write about independence, or, more obviously, organize or fight for independence.

Of her mother's war years, Sotomayor says, "She speaks about the burdens in her life in fragments and only sparingly."[9] Given

that she spoke little English and was unfamiliar with how tele-
phones worked, or why she had to wear a mask in the gas chamber, we might guess why a colonial subject like Báez would want
to leave all that was familiar for an alternative premised on hope.
And what survives about her story in the official record? Inciden-
tals, and silence mostly. It could mistakenly be reduced to an
anecdote devoid of historical context, as Sotomayor has done in
her memoir and in her public renderings of her mother's life: a
seventeen-year-old girl, alone, without a soul to rely on, and not
knowing English, leaves the island for "a better life." In such a
story, to say "Celina Báez" is to say "sacrifice." But perhaps we
would do well to remember that story better. If you left the
island, as Celina Báez did on the heels of World War II (1939–45),
you might hope that if you ever did have children, they wouldn't
have a country to remember or homeland to betray. Nostalgia is
an expensive proposition when all you want to do is forget what
you've left behind. But when you can't forget, because the memory of dispersal included how to use a gas mask in a language
that was not your mother tongue, you might simply reference
that story "in fragments and only sparingly," as Sotomayor has
said of her mother's recollection of her colonial migration to the
mainland at seventeen. If the mediapheme that we've inherited
about Sotomayor's personal life is cautious about personal disclosure, and what little we know about the story of her mother's war
years, we can be certain to know even less about Sotomayor's
father, Juan Luis Sotomayor (1921–1963). Understood in terms of
absences, displacements, and fragments, Sotomayor's family history reads like a story of colonial hauntings.

At the opening of El Museo del Barrio's "Nueva York: 1613–
1945," Sotomayor delivered the keynote to the exhibit, which was
touted as the first to reveal "the powerful role that Latinos and

Spanish-speaking countries have played over three centuries to help shape New York into the most culturally vibrant city in the world."[10] Sotomayor acknowledged that the exhibit itself allowed her to learn more about the plight of her father, who died when she was only nine years old, and how he eventually met Báez in New York City. She said that conversations with her mother made her realize that Juan Luis Sotomayor had left Puerto Rico "aboard the *SS George S. Simmons*," and she jokingly added, "I thought everyone came by airplane" (see website, figure 5). Sotomayor repeated a version of this in her memoir, where she wrote that the ship in question was the *George S. Simonds* (1942–46), a recommissioned army transport ship whose first incarnation was as the *Great Northern* passenger steamer. The *Great Northern* was acquired by the navy in 1917 when the United States entered WW I, and by the time the Great War was over, it had transported over twenty-eight thousand soldiers to war across the Atlantic. It is with some irony that we should note that the *Great Northern* was the first to transport Puerto Rican soldiers to the European theater of war before it was recommissioned as the army transport ship—the *George S. Simonds*—that brought Sotomayor's father from San Juan to New York. When the *George S. Simmonds* brought Juan Luis Sotomayor to New York, the ship had already sent a generation of Puerto Ricans to their fate. By the time Juan Luis Sotomayor left Puerto Rico, the U.S. Army had recommissioned the *Great Northern* as the *George S. Simmonds* transport ship that was used during World War II to reshuffle the stagnant labor force from the island to the states.

Sotomayor has noted many times in her story of social mobility through sacrifice that her father had left the island to find work stateside because of Puerto Rico's dire economic predicament at the time, which was augmented by World War II. As the most densely populated territory in the world, it was a laboratory for biological experimentation, sterilization, and a truncated representative democracy impoverished through "tax-exempt free commerce" for U.S. corporations after the island was surrendered to U.S. military authority through the Foraker Act in 1900. But why would a young man who worked as an auto mechanic in the Santurce district of Puerto Rico's capital leave the island in the middle of World War II, during the second major conscription of Puerto Ricans, when everyone from technicians to proletarian farmers to the unemployed were sent to war? With the war effort in full force, only men under eighteen, the "feeble," and the disabled were exempted. At the start of World War II, in 1939, Juan Luis Sotomayor would have been eighteen years old.

The Santurce registrar of births is closed most any day you want to go during the week. In an annex to the municipal hall for the capital in San Juan, you wait in a line that overflows from the building to the sidewalk. The longer-than-usual wait times began when Homeland Security officers started supervising all transactions after some municipal employees began selling the birth certificates of recently deceased Puerto Ricans to Latin American immigrants, often from the Dominican Republic, who want to come to United States. "Paciencia joven" (Patience, young man) is what I hear from the man who recognizes me after several visits, or, "No se apure señorito" (Don't rush yourself, delicate sir), from those who have sized up my queer impatience. And after complaining about waiting in line to whoever will hear me out after my sixth visit, a woman within earshot says, "¿Los Sotomayor? Véte a Lares." Go to Lares, she tells me. And so I do. Lares, home of the Grito de Lares, the first uprising in the Puerto Rican independence movement, reveals a history of forgetting and loss beyond the impoverished imaginings of the Sotomayor media spectacles reproduced in the press after her nomination to the Supreme Court. The surname Sotomayor in Lares carries a particular resonance on the island that does not often translate to the mainland, though it should.

PUERTO RICAN COLONIAL ARCHIVES

One of the first Sotomayors to garner national attention in the mid-twentieth century was the Puerto Rican Nationalist and independence leader Gonzalo Lebrón Sotomayor. After arriving in the states from Puerto Rico in the 1940s, Lebrón Sotomayor was deemed a threat to national security given his work with Nationalists on the island. He quickly rose through the leadership ranks of the Puerto Rican Nationalist Party, and in the early 1950s he became president of the party's Chicago branch. President Eisenhower's FBI kept him under surveillance, as it did anyone suspected of being a Puerto Rican Nationalist or sympathizer; especially stateside. He was ultimately co-opted and, according to evidence released through Freedom of Information Act (FOIA), turned state's evidence against his sister, the far better known Puerto Rican independence leader Dolores "Lolita" Lebrón Sotomayor (1919—2010).[11] Dolores, from el Barrio de Bartoló de Lares, was most commonly known as Lolita to her contemporaries while she was alive, or as Doña Lolita to the young on the island and stateside who have made an icon of this other Sotomayor. Dolores, or Lolita as she came to be known, was Albizu Campos's second in command and, alternately, the leader of the Puerto Rican Nationalist Party during Albizu Campos's various incarcerations. While there is no evidence that there is a direct relationship between Juan Luis Sotomayor and Gonzalo Lebrón Sotomayor or his sister, Lolita, the history that the surname indexes nonetheless points to key chapters of colonial violence that led to both Celina Báez's and Juan Luis Sotomayor's colonial migration to the states. That history of colonial violence against Puerto Rican demands for autonomy and independence from colonial rule should be understood in opposition to the states of debt required for entry into the nation's civic life, and it requires a deep accounting.

The independence movement first gained a political stronghold in Puerto Rico after World War I. This was partly because of the tax-exempt status granted to U.S. corporations on the island, which impoverished Puerto Rico's infrastructure both in terms of extractive capital campaigns, and as evidenced by lives lost after Puerto Rican soldiers were conscripted for the first theater of war in World War I and subsequently. Island tax exemptions for U.S. corporations both impoverished the island's infrastructure and prevented locals from earning anything remotely resembling a living wage. Joining the armed forces, by choice or through conscription, was a way to make a living, even if that living could potentially end your life. For example, by the time Celina Báez and Juan Luis Sotomayor left in the early 1940s, almost 50 percent of the island's inhabitants were infected with tuberculosis, malaria, or hookworm, and only two of the island's seventy-seven districts had doctors. The situation was so dire that from 1930 onward the forced sterilization of women was seen as a viable public health solution by colonial authorities. Indeed, Sanger herself stated as early as 1932 that some populations simply should not reproduce. She was referring to Puerto Rico. The festering resentment that had already crystallized after World War I led to a more staunchly confrontational and vocal independence movement. As noted, quite late in this history Law 53 codified what the colonial authorities had been doing since the 1920s: censoring internal dissent through the detention and, in some instances, torture and disappearance of political insurgents. Largely in response to this, the Nationalist Party proper was established in 1922. Under the leadership of Albizu Campos, the Nationalist Party began to stage public events that were meant to call attention to Puerto Rico's occupation and to the extralegal detention of Nationalists by colonial authorities during this heightened state of exception.

As early as 1930, the Nationalists under the leadership of Albizu Campos publicly accused the colonial regime of torturing Nationalist Party members. In particular, Albizu Campos began to decry a series of radiation experiments that he alleged were being conducted on Nationalist political prisoners as well as on unwitting participants, usually recruited from the rural countryside, by the Rockefeller Foundation under the guise of various public health and rural rehabilitation initiatives. Albizu Campos considered these alleged clandestine activities to be part of a broader "race extermination plot" perpetuated against the Puerto Rican people by the United States. Since 1932, Albizu Campos had singled out Dr. Cornelius P. Rhoads. Rhoads was a medical doctor and researcher who worked for the Rockefeller Foundation in Puerto Rico. Albizu Campos charged that Rhoads heaped abuse on Puerto Ricans as a group and claimed to have killed several through radiation poisoning and "injecting cancer into several more," all in his capacity as a physician. Albizu Campos made these charges based on a letter by Rhoads obtained by the Nationalists with the help of one of Rhoads's technicians, Luis Baldoni, a Nationalist sympathizer. The letter reads in part,

Puerto Ricans are beyond doubt the dirtiest, laziest, most degener-
ate and thievish race of men ever inhabiting this sphere. It makes
you sick to inhabit the same island with them. They are even lower
than Italians. What the island needs is not public health work but a
tidal wave or something to totally exterminate the population. It
might then be livable. I have done my best to further the process of
extermination by killing off 8 and transplanting cancer into several
more.[12]

Since it was impossible to deny the existence of the letter once it
was made public by the Nationalists, the Rockefeller Foundation hired Ivy Ledbetter Lee, considered the founder of modern
public relations, to manage the incident. In various newspaper
reports, Rhoads repeated the same soundbite: that the letter was
"never intended to mean [anything] other than the opposite of
what was stated."[13] The island's U.S.-appointed governor, James
R. Beverly (1894–1967), exonerated Rhoads and accepted the
researcher's apology for his "unfortunate joke."[14] The outcome
of the investigation was ultimately crucial to Rhoads's career.
He went on to serve as the director of the Sloan Kettering Institute for Cancer Research thanks to his research on the use of
radiation as an effective treatment against cancer. Indeed,
Rhoads established the standard radiation protocols in human
subjects that made him a pioneer in cancer research by deter-
mining the threshold for radiation poisoning in humans.

The Rhoads incident marked the emergence of a more
directly confrontational Nationalist resistance that included the
planned assassination of colonial authorities and, eventually, the
U.S. president. Colonial authorities had early on infiltrated the
Nationalist Party, and Albizu Campos was eventually detained
and taken to the infamous La Princesa Penitentiary in Old San
Juan, where, as Nationalist prisoners had alleged since the early

1930s, they were subjected to illegal detention, torture, and medical experimentation. There is testimonial evidence that Nationalist detainees would be sedated and taken from La Princesa to Presbyterian Hospital in San Juan for "medical care" under Rhoads's watch up to 1932. In a stunning confluence of irony, imperial science, and the biomanagement of subaltern populations, Albizu Campos's own life begins to take on the semblance and structure of a magical realist narrative shortly after his second prolonged incarceration in late 1950. He alleged then that he himself was the victim of radiological experimentation, his first exposure occurring on February 1, 1951. After his second alleged exposure on March 9 of that same year, he claimed to have endured eight more treatments from late 1951 to early 1953. With the help of sympathetic guards, Nationalists arranged to have Albizu Campos's irradiated body photographed (see author website, figure 6).

The image literalized the colonial violence enacted on both the leader of the Nationalist Party and the broader Puerto Rican body politic. The evidentiary demands of the visual narrative that inhere in Albizu Campos's defeated body bears an indexical relationship to the corporeal landscape it would appear to mimic by literalizing the territorial subjection of Puerto Rico under colonial rule. The cracks and crevices on Albizu Campos's swollen skin allegorized the costs associated with colonial resistance. The image, of course, did not circulate in the United States, though Cuban and Mexican newspapers did publish it as exemplary visual evidence of "Yankee imperialism," further associating the Nationalist cause with an emergent red scare that simply obviated the organizing principles of the Nationalist Party. These were organized around God, home, family, and, eventually, nation-state, as the autonomous space for the integration of these founding conceits, certainly not a "God free" Marxist Puerto Rico. Indeed, the centrality of God, home, and family as the inexorable progenitors of nation were grounded on the figuration of the child as the principal emblem of a possible national future always under the literal threat of extermination through the already well-documented forced-sterilization campaign against rural women in Puerto Rico. This understandable distrust culminated in one of the most fascinating yet underanalyzed moments in the convergence of the women's liberation movement as it came to be understood in the late 1960s and its relation the story of the lived experience of Puerto Rican subalternity under colonial rule.

BIOPOLITICS AND OTHER PUERTO RICAN COLONIAL HAUNTINGS

Emerging out of the forced sterilization of rural women, planning for clandestine contraceptive pill trials began in Puerto Rico in 1952. Correspondence between researchers John Rock, Gregory Pincus, and their associates, as well as Margaret Sanger, their principal financial supporter, suggest that they had considered Puerto Rico an ideal setting for human trials early on. This is significant. Pincus visited Puerto Rico and determined that it would be the perfect location. The island had all the human and structural ingredients they had hoped for. In one of his letters to Sanger, Pincus noted that there were no anti–birth control laws on the books and that the island had an extensive network of metropolitan and rural clinics. Indeed, there were sixty-seven clinics dispensing existing methods of birth control, and many women used their services, which included training on "the rhythm method" for birth control. The massive sterilization of Puerto Rican women was a well-known fact to Rock, Pincus, and Sanger, who had promoted it in her *Birth Control Review*.

Sanger knew that eventual public outcry would make sterilization for population control undesirable in the long run. With Rock and Pincus, she also knew that if Puerto Rico's "baby machines," as she referred to Puerto Rican women, could be trained to stay on a contraceptive regimen, then it would be more profitable than forced sterilization from both the financial and the public relations angle. They hoped to demonstrate that if Puerto Rican women could successfully use oral contraceptives, they would quiet concerns that oral contraceptives would be too "complicated" for women in developing nations and, as Sanger often noted in her speeches, in America's inner cities. After Pincus visited the island in the early 1950s, he saw it as an ideal place for the clandestine trials, using the first hormonal birth control pill, Enovid. The clinical trials for what eventually became the contraceptive pill took place in Puerto Rico because Pincus and Sanger determined that it would be "too problematic" to carry them out stateside. Puerto Rico proved to be the "perfect" place to determine both the efficacy and the dosage of Enovid. Puerto Rican women from rural areas and the countryside were recruited and given formulations of the drug without being told they were serving as test subjects, or, in common parlance, guinea pigs. There is evidence that Puerto Rican women died during the clandestine test phase of the experiments, though their deaths would never be investigated.[15] The Food and Drug Administration finally approved "the pill" in 1960 and in so doing ushered in the modern women's liberation movement at the expense of Puerto Rican women. The lasting effects of using Puerto Rico as a laboratory are almost as astounding as the limited research and related historical colonial silences surrounding U.S. imperial domination of the island. (It cannot be understated that pharmaceutical and bio-experimentation on the island with Enovid and related estrogens led to the contamination of foodways, which in turn has made Puerto Rico one of the world's centers for "premature sexual development" and "sexual indeterminacy.")[16] Albizu Campos and the Nationalists were well aware of the forced sterilizations and biological experimentation on the island undertaken against Puerto Ricans. In his speeches, letters, and archival material, it is clear that he understood that such experimentation to be the literal annihilation of the Puerto Rican people. Since his second incarceration, from 1950 to 1953, he had been corresponding with Lolita Lebrón, that is, Dolores Lebrón Sotomayor.

Given the interception of communiqués and the fear of reprisals, they began fashioning in their correspondence a highly effective poetic language that was couched in the cultural and Christian symbology they both shared. Lebrón wrote to Albizu Campus while he was in jail, and it is clear from their exchanges that they meant to encode Nationalist intentions in the biblical shorthand of the epistle. Invoking the Book of Mathew, she wrote to Albizu Campos about a dream of hers in which Puerto Rico was where *el masacre de los inocentes*, "the massacre of the innocents," had taken place. In Matthew's New Testament telling of Jeramiah's prophecy, the story of King Herod's slaughter of children in Bethlehem unfolds after a dream foretold of the child savior's birth. King Herod "sent forth and put to death all the male children who were in Bethlehem and in all its districts, from two years old and under" (Matthew 2:16). Lebrón's symbolic shorthand indicates the extent to which the Nationalists felt they were under the sign of Saturn, the Roman god who devoured his own children at birth for fear of being displaced by them. Indeed, given the level of heightened suppression of Nationalist activity, including writing, theater, performance, or anything deemed critical of U.S. colonial authorities, Lebrón resorted to poetry as a way to escape censorship under the Law of the Muzzle. In one of the most famous poem-prophecies, "A Message from God in the Atomic Age," she recounts that "God had spoken" to her in order to warn others through her of the United States' imminent destruction of Puerto Rico. Her "prophetic divination" poems made manifest how U.S. imperial power would signal the end of the world as we know it. Many of these poems and verses were composed while she herself was incarcerated, and they extended in poetic language what she had communicated with Albizu Campos in her telegraphed epistolary exchanges. A collection of these poems was published shortly after she was pardoned by the Jimmy Carter administration under the title *Sándalo en la celda* (Sandalwood in the cell, 1975).[17] Though the history of the prophetic attack on Congress is known, this prehistory is not.

The better-known official record is more prosaic. The Lolita Lebrón mediapheme, if it survives at all, has been reduced to the date of March 1, 1954. Along with Nationalists Rafael Cancel Miranda, Irving Flores, and Andres Figueroa Cordero, she entered the U.S. House of Representatives, the "People's House" of government, armed with guns. Accounts note that before opening fire, she draped herself in the Puerto Rican flag and entered a palace of sorts—the governing body that could take citizenship from Puerto Ricans as easily as it conferred it at the end of World War I—and she shouted, perhaps in uneasy English, "Freedom for Puerto Rico!" And then she pulled a pistol from her purse and began shooting. The five shots from her pistol ricocheted though the chamber in protest of Puerto Rico's occupation by the United States. This moment in history made Dolores Lebrón Sotomayor the "Lolita" we know today. And while that rendering has also made her a radiant icon of colonial resistance to her followers, she continues to be largely an ignored footnote to American history as the woman who led "the first terrorist attack on U.S. soil." No one was killed, though she was later sentenced to twenty-five years in prison, serving most of her time in Alderston, West Virginia. In late 1954, Albizu Campos was again incarcerated and sentenced to ten years for masterminding the attack that Lebrón led in Washington, DC. Pardoned again in 1964 due to international pressure, Albizu Campos died months after his release in 1965. Even after Lolita Lebrón's eventual release from prison after she was pardoned, her political convictions never wavered. In her eighties she was arrested again and served sixty days in jail for protesting an American military base on the island of Vieques in Puerto Rico. Dolores "Lolita" Lebrón Sotomayor died August 1, 2010. It was the year Sonia Sotomayor completed her first term on the Supreme Court of the United States.

INDENTURED JUNK BONDING:
THE NEOLIBERAL SACKING OF PUERTO RICO

Hurricane Maria devastated Puerto Rico when it made landfall on the island on September 20, 2017. Shortly after, Sonia Sotomayor recorded a message of hope in Spanish to the residents of Puerto Rico in the aftermath of the devastation and the Trump administration's complicity in the collapse of the island's infrastructure. Titled "Message to Puerto Rico," it was broadcast on Puerto Rico's WKAQ 580 and later transcribed and published in English. It read,

This past week I've felt especially connected to my Puerto Rican brethren here and those on our beloved island. I'm grateful that I was able to hear from many in my family. But I know that many other people are still going through uncertainty as they await to receive news from their loved ones.

Our hearts are anguished in the face of so much devastation and destruction that [Hurricane] María caused. And now we face the great task of reconstruction. But above all, we are united in the firm belief that Puerto Rico will persevere. The incredible spirit and strength of the Puerto Rican people is unbreakable. Our island has faced innumerable challenges throughout the centuries. However, each and every time, Puerto Rico has emerged stronger. And we will do so again.

For the people on the island, I want you to know that you are not alone. Your families and friends, along with private and public organizations, have already begun to mobilize to send help. Through our ability to work hard, the *Isla del Encanto* will be reborn as a beacon of hope. Puerto Rico will not only survive this. It will bloom once again. My beloved Puerto Rico, I embrace you with love and hope. I hope to see you in a not-so-distant future.[18]

While hope and encouragement became Sotomayor's signal offering to the devastated island, much as departing the island was all Celina Báez could hope for herself, it seemed as if she had given up on her earlier emphasis on legally structuring Puerto Rico's political independence from the United States by reducing its economic dependence on it. As a law student at Yale, for example, Sotomayor wrote her first article in the *Yale Law Review* on Puerto Rican seabed rights. In this initial law school note, Sotomayor attempted to find a legal way for Puerto Rico to own its natural resources, if not on land, then in the island's surrounding seabed. After the destruction caused by Hurricane Maria on the island's infrastructure, and the resulting shock to human resiliency in its aftermath, offering hope and love seemed necessary but was also a stark compromise compared with her earlier academic exercise.

Nearly a year after Hurricane Maria destroyed Puerto Rico's infrastructure, President Trump cast doubt on the official estimates of deaths resulting from the hurricane. In a series of tweets, Trump insisted that there were no more than "eighteen deaths" and that it was all a hoax by "Democrats in order to make me look bad." Beyond the blatant falsehood, empirically contradicted by researchers at George Washington University and later Harvard, the goal was simple. The lower the number of "official" deaths, the less insurance companies would have to cover for indemnified loss of life *and* property losses (construction and rebuilding from scratch is a profit industry the president is well versed in). Additionally, by not counting deaths as disaster related, the Federal Emergency Management Agency would not have to pay for funerary costs, as required under federal rules.[19] According to an initial report from George Washington University's Milken Institute School of Public Health, the death toll related to Hurricane Maria was an estimated 2,975. A later report from Harvard's T.H. Chan School of Public Health lists the number of deaths as 4,645.

It is clear that neither properly accounting for Puerto Rican deaths nor grieving the dead is allowed in the final debt-credit analysis of the island's ties to the United States. Emblematic of the sacking of post-Maria Puerto Rico was the "Cocktails and Compliance" party organized in Old San Juan for venture capitalists—also known as "vulture capitalists"—to learn how to "safely" invest in the island after the hurricane. In 2012, during the Obama presidency, the Puerto Rican Legislative Assembly passed two laws intended to make the island a "global investment destination." After Hurricane Maria razed the island, the "vulture capitalists" saw the 2012 laws as an investment opportunity. One of these, Act 20, allowed corporations that export services from the island to pay only a 4 percent operations tax. The other, Act 22, makes Puerto Rico the only territory in the United States where personal income from capital gains, interest, and dividends goes completely untaxed. After the 2012 law vulture capitalists no longer had to give up their U.S. passports to hide their assets abroad. Hurricane Maria's razing of the island created the clean slate for the latest capital-extraction campaign. It would appear that even the dead cannot rest in peace in Puerto Rico. It is now clear that what was left of their resting place no longer belongs to Puerto Ricans, dead or alive. To paraphrase Walter Benjamin's dictum from his "Theses on the Philosophy of History" (1940), even the dead are not be safe from extractive capitalists. We must therefore endeavor to create a politics that can name the dead, as well as the culpable, a politics of redress that stands witness by those who mourn on the edge of democracy's graveyard.

Sotomayor's life story, enacted through narrative appeals to an ostensibly postrace American dream of inclusion, requires a series of sacrifices and unspeakable collusions that evacuate the complexity of living within a national discourse of inclusion incapable of embracing the dirty and complex work of historical accountability. In such a narrative, the motherland, Celina Báez, ultimately requires losing history for a seat at the table; Juan Luis Sotomayor, the fatherland, becomes the unassimilable historical supplement. And thus the problem with representative personhood for "Latinos," as it is understood in the public imagination. "See," the Sotomayor mediapheme implores at its best, "if she can do it, so can you." A reverse salvo of the *¡Sí se puede!* that so many of us have been fighting for, runs the risk of leaving us unable to make clear why an appeal for political enfranchisement under the rubric of a collective identity binds us to a history of representative personhood incapable of addressing how our differences and contributions need to be made intelligible in the public sphere. The prospect of having to do so might require losing Sonia Sotomayor. Not the person, or the impressive accomplishments that make her so appealing, but the belief in the benevolence of the state to embrace us as the "Latinos" the state thinks we are.

Refusing to believe in the state's benevolence allows us to awaken from an elusive national fantasy incapable of reciprocating our differences and the histories that subtend those differences. Such are the limits and responsibilities of *being Brown* in our moment, forsaking the mediapheme, even in its most positive and seductive incarnations, in order to awaken from the elusive—albeit seductive—dream of inclusion. Ignoring that history erases the historical specificity that can explain Puerto Rican citizenship as exceptional within the U.S. Latino body politic and the history of U.S. empire building at home and beyond. Most importantly, understanding Sotomayor as a representative Latina ultimately absolves our national institutions of accounting for why our democracy has failed such a demographically significant component of the American body politic at most every historical juncture, and why Puerto Rico's history must be understood as intimately tied to U.S. empire building as a primary site of continuous capital extraction campaigns.

As the reigning economic paradigm, austerity establishes basic principles—the shrinking of government, spending less, and refusing to forgive debt—that serve as useful analogues to Sotomayor's story of financial, historical, colonial, and cultural indebtedness. Beyond mere biographical interest in the first

Latina Supreme Court associate justice, we would do well to remember how stories of ethnic and racial economic mobility in alt-right times affect and guide public policy, educational agendas, and our collective understanding of what I've called the Latino question. When we examine the Sotomayor mediapheme, when we learn to distinguish the symbol of inclusion for the complex story it purportedly represents, we come to realize that the Latino question is far from answered, not even topically understood.

Though the evidence is all around us— the dead bodies abound—it is tempting nonetheless to look away and understand this rhetorical substitution as proof of an unprecedented postracial shift from institutional and national exclusion to the incorporation of Latinos. But de jure discrimination, limited access to educational opportunities, a broken immigration system, and the unaccounted-for dead—to name but a few historical flashpoints—all put the lie to the much-exaggerated entry of the Latino body into American civic life. Because that is an odious debt—one whose dividends are not meant for us—we must insist on the historical accounting that might liberate us, just long enough, to free ourselves from its death grip so that we may in turn breathe, live, resist and create a just Brown commons.

Thinking Otherwise

Sonia Sotomayor and the Emergence
of Latino Legal Thought

Can jurisprudence, the philosophy and theory of the law, be said to have an ethnic, racial, or gender identity? The U.S. Supreme Court, and the justices who are the living embodiment of the institution, must perform as if the answer to this question were an unequivocal *no.* The Supreme Court is, as established in the U.S. Constitution, the final arbiter of laws passed by Congress, and it is the institutional body entrusted to be the final judge of the nation's highest laws. Its task is ultimately one of interpretation, and therein lies the importance of Supreme Court appointments. Supreme Court appointments are for life, and in a political culture in which Congress is dysfunctional and incapable of legislating, as evidenced by the most recent and longest government shutdown of 2018–19, the Supreme Court is often seen as "legislating laws," which should be the provenance of the legislative branch of government, rather than "applying the law," which is its ostensible purpose. The performance of "impartiality" therefore requires disavowals at most every turn. As we saw in chapter 1, for universalists the law is impartial a priori and therefore color-blind and value-neutral; ergo any consideration of ethnic, gendered, or racial particularisms is simply an untenable proposition unworthy of discussion. For both universalists and Supreme Court justices, then, the answer to my opening question is also a resounding *no,* since they believe in an ecumenical standard, above and beyond individual or group differences. The reality, of course, is quite different insofar as certain social out-groups bear the violent brunt of the law's reach in ways that belie such universalist logics. And therein lies the rub: the reach of "justice" is disproportionately felt by those ethnic subjects who are always already within its reach, putting legal impartiality to its ultimate test on the body of the other. That is what makes Sonia Sotomayor's juridical thinking so fascinating for me. After nearly a decade of Sotomayor's tenure on the Supreme Court, we can now assess her record through her jurisprudential thinking as evidenced in her legal opinions, dissents, and lectures, as well as in her own public humanities work. In this closing chapter my goal is to foreground some of Sotomayor's most important engagements with what I am here calling "Latino legal thought." My purpose is not exhaustive. Rather, I hope to chart how thinking otherwise might allow us to better imagine the futures of *being Brown* in the democratic commons.

As we saw in chapter 3, the Sotomayor mediapheme cast her as, among many things, a liberal "reverse racist." Based on what came to be known as her "wise Latina" speech from 2001, the Sotomayor mediapheme ultimately made the evidence of her judicial thinking subservient to the use value of her persona as circulated through diverse political media. As I noted previously, New York senator Charles Schumer stated the obvious: while she was on the U.S. Court of Appeals for the Second Circuit from 1998 to 2009, her record consisted of over three thousand cases and nearly four hundred opinions that aligned her judicial thinking with conservative ideologies and outcomes. Schumer's strategy, of course, was to rehabilitate Sotomayor's professed lack of "impartiality," which meant that her juridical thinking had to yield results similar to those of white male judges, who are a priori presumed to be "impartial." The facts that Schumer strategically presented did just that. Sotomayor's judicial thinking was aligned with desired conservative results. How could such an ostensibly "impartial," "universalist," and "color-blind" record with a preponderance of evidence favoring majority defendants over and against minorities be reconciled with the public persona that she was a "racist" activist judge? I believe that despite the juridical thinking evinced in Sotomayor's decisions and opinions before her confirmation, we can now evaluate her thinking as a Supreme Court associate justice whose intellectual prowess is at its peak. I also believe that based on the evidence now at hand, we can indeed answer how Sotomayor would respond to the question that frames this closing chapter: also a calculated *no*. But before explaining why she must perform her "impartiality," it would be useful to ground the basis for a provisional definition of what I'm here calling "Latino legal thought."

LATINO LEGAL THOUGHT IN CONTEXT

It is with some irony that constitutional "originalists," those who believe that the meaning of the Constitution does not change or evolve over time, along with "textualists," those who are also originalists but give primary weight to the intention of the text and structure of the Constitution, somehow have to contend with the "disparate impact" protections of the 1964 Civil Rights Act, which prohibit discrimination, among many other things, on the basis of race and sex. Not far behind these in degrees of irony are the "intentionalists," who are, you guessed it, also originalists who give primary weight to the intention of the Constitution's framers, ratifiers, and foundational dissenters who have bequeathed through their writing their disagreements with particular elements of the Constitution. Adding to the foundational deference evinced in these interpretive positions, I note a final irony: the original framers at the Convention in Philadelphia indicated that they did not want their specific intentions to control future interpretations. Regardless, the Supreme Court remains packed with justices who may vary on what they give primary weight to while interpreting the highest law of the land but who are nonetheless unabashed originalists. That is, they are beholden to the words, intent, and original purpose of the country's slaveholding founders. Now back to the future. Outside the originalist core on the current Supreme Court we also have the "pragmatists." Ruth Bader Ginsburg and Sonia Sotomayor are the most prominent. Elena Kagan, who arrived on the court as Obama's second nominee, was confirmed in 2010 and can also be considered a legal pragmatist. These pragmatists give substantial weight to stare decisis, that is, judicial precedent, all the while plotting the consequences of potential interpretations. While there are other areas of focus and related interpretive frames, the four I have briefly described encapsulate generally accepted modes of interpretation for the best-known constitutional scholars currently on the court.[1]

As we saw in my discussion of *Hernández v. Texas,* the legal concept of "disparate impact" refers to institutional practices in education, housing, employment, and other areas that adversely affect people from protected groups that have historically faced discrimination. The groups generally identified as falling under "a class status" are protected according to the group member's race, color, religion, national origin, sex, and disability status, or some combination thereof. The 1964 Civil Rights Act, discussed in chapter 3, provides remedy for violations under its Title VII protections for these protected classes if it can be proved that a practice or policy has a disproportionately adverse effect on these groups. Related legislation and corresponding amendments and laws, aimed at protecting minorities from discrimination, have addressed well-known historical injustices, and it is in this sense that we can affirm that the Civil Rights Act has provided the most significant set of civil rights protections since Reconstruction. But just how effective have these protections been for Latinos?

The answer is not much. So much for the impartially of the law. Writing in the late 1990s, legal studies scholar Jean Stefancic noted that "much of U.S. antidiscrimination law has not served the needs of Latinos."[2] Stefancic explains,

> Not only has progress been halting, but court decisions and policy choices have been unreliable and wavering. Reparational civil rights law, based on a black/white paradigm and crafted to address historical injustice against African Americans, has not always worked as effectively for Latinos, especially those defined by multiple categories.[3]

For Stefancic, the practice of reparational justice has been mired in a Manichean, Black-and-white dichotomy that continues to render Latinos invisible as a distinct class. Despite the 1954 *Hernández v. Texas* Supreme Court decision, as well as the array of various other protections extended after, it is the application of antidiscrimination law that thwarts the possibility of achieving a meaningfully cogent reparative justice for Latino subjects. Many of these concerns led to the creation in 1995 of what came to be known in legal studies scholarship as Latino Critical Theory, or "LatCrit Theory" for short. LatCrit Theory evolved from Critical Race Theory and consolidated in 1995 through the agency of a handful of legal studies scholars, as well as other scholars in Chicano, African American, gender and sexuality, and Latino studies, who were concerned about how both legal education and the discourse of law had perpetuated the continued invisibility of Latinos in three spheres: law education and training, jurisprudential thinking, and criminal justice praxis. Francisco Valdes, one of the foundational figures of LatCrit, explained that it "is a scholarly movement responding to the long historical presence and enduring invisibility of Latinas/os in the lands now known as the United States."[4] He notes that as a "method,"

> the "LatCrit" approach to law and theory, to justice and society, includes a collection of principles and practices that have been assembled largely, though not exclusively, from two main sources: the prior jurisprudential experiments of "critical legal studies" and associated movements; and eight years of experience with the "LatCrit" experiment, which began in 1995. As shaped by these principles and practices, LatCrit theory, praxis and community represent individual and collective commitments to the vindication of civil and human rights globally.[5]

As described by Valdes, LatCrit is attuned to difference as a way of thinking and doing in the world through jurisprudence and as a means to make manifest how difference is both paradoxically inscribed and made either visible or invisible in and through legal discourse. As such, it is not a stretch to concede that LatCrit jurisprudential thinking is an attempt at formulating a Brown commons in and through the discourse of law. Now, more than a quarter century after its inception, do we have any evidence of LatCrit's influence on the Supreme Court? The answer here is also a resounding *no*. Given the nature of the court, it is doubtful that we would ever be able to respond affirmatively, for the very legitimacy of the Supreme Court is related to its insistence on the very color-blind impartiality that LatCrit would contest. We can, however, discern—without making correlational attribution—that the embodiment of difference in the figure of Sotomayor may in fact be making such a difference in the way the court understands and acts on the question of Latino difference. For the purpose of this heuristic proposition, I am here defining "Latino legal thought" as, first, jurisprudence that either recognizes or acknowledges Latino ethnic particularisms as experienced in and through the criminal justice system, and, second, as the clear expression of those particularisms as articulated in established or emerging case law. We might consider this, again invoking the work of José Esteban Muñoz, as "thinking otherwise."

THINKING OTHERWISE

Sotomayor did not have an easy first year on the court. It's a difficult adjustment, and everyone's eyes and ears are on you in ways even a seasoned jurist such as Sotomayor would find overwhelming. And not all her colleagues were welcoming. The late Antonin Scalia (1936–2016), avowed textualist and son of Trenton, New Jersey, did not like Sotomayor. The feeling was mutual. Early on, as news of potential nominees emerged to replace David Souter, Scalia told Obama adviser David Axelrod at a White House Correspondents' Association Dinner that he had "no illusions that your man [Obama] will nominate someone who shares my orientation."[6] But nonetheless he told Axelrod, point blank, "I hope he sends us someone smart." With characteristic bravado, Scalia was to the point when he had Axelrod's ear. "I hope he sends us Elena Kagan," he said. But he got Sotomayor instead, and "Nino," as Scalia was affectionately called by those close to him, was not happy about that. Sotomayor would not be a friend. Between the two there was, if not enmity, certainly a sustained tension. During her second year on the court, for example, Sotomayor attended a Christmas-caroling event that Scalia hosted every year. After a few carols, Scalia asked Sotomayor if she had any requests. She did. Her offering was a Christmas classic written by Puerto Rican musician José Feliciano. She said, "Feliz Navidad," but Scalia's tone was admonishing. "We don't sing *that* song at this party." The disciplining of Sotomayor by Scalia was likely instructive. The hospitable invitation offered by Scalia, only to be withdrawn, was undoubtedly not as symbolic for Scalia as it was for Sotomayor. But the incident is emblematic of the transition of Sotomayor from a conservative pro-government juridical thinker to a Sotomayor marked by a juridical "otherwiseness" that merits commentary. For Muñoz "thinking otherwise" was a way of marking how philosophical reasoning should not be "reserved for subjects who claim a more objectivist mode of knowledge production and knowing."[7] But just what might that thinking otherwise look like in practice?

Sotomayor has lived many firsts, from being the first in her family to graduate from college, to being the first Supreme Court Latina associate justice, to being the first Supreme Court member to describe herself as a Latina. In the history of the Supreme Court, she is also the first to inscribe "undocumented immigrant" over and above the more commonplace designation of its politically charged predecessor, "illegal immigrant." Eschewing "illegal" as a designation for human beings, as well as the legally

imprecise term "Hispanic," she made history quietly but genera-
tively. Sotomayor authored her first opinion on December 8, 2009,
in *Mohawk Industries, Inc. v. Carpenter,* a case involving whether
attorney-client privilege could be appealed. The case concerned
an employee of Mohawk Industries who had complained to the
human resources department that the company was hiring "illegal immigrants." The employee was instructed to meet with a
company lawyer, who allegedly pressured the employee to recant
the statement. The employee, however, did not recant and was
subsequently fired. In the ensuing litigation the employee sought
information from the company regarding his meeting with the
company lawyer, but the company asserted attorney-client privilege and confidentiality. The federal district court ordered
Mohawk to disclose the information and concurrently allowed
Mohawk to appeal. At stake was whether disclosure orders that
are adverse to attorney-client privilege qualify for immediate
appeal.

Sotomayor's majority opinion held that it did not constitute
attorney-client privilege, and this was consequential for two reasons. First, it did not foreclose the possibility that litigant whistle-
blowers could make claims, substantiated or not, that seek retribution against undocumented workers through employers.
Second, paradoxically, the case also allowed for another level of
political representation to emerge in civil society and related
legal discourses. That is, by inscribing "undocumented immigrant" on the official court record, the category itself emerged *as
if* it were a protected class. The broader meaning of her first
opinion was significant. In a sense, she was overturning precedent by breaking with the designation "illegal immigrant" and
instead using "undocumented immigrant." In so doing, Sotomayor
upended the accepted, "reasonable" assumption that an individu-

al's entire social identity can be designated through law as fundamentally "illegal." Sotomayor's distinction was significant insofar as it acknowledged that an action or a *doing* may be illegal under the law, but a human being cannot be delimited by an action. The *Mohawk Industries, Inc. v. Carpenter* case effectively allowed her to perform the immigrant activists' salvo "No human being is illegal" while, not inconsequentially, disavowing the question of impartiality. In so doing, Sotomayor asserted a maxim of Critical Race Theory rarely acknowledged outside academic settings: social identities and their relationships to law matter, because the law will not release these identities. Examples abound. From slavery to Jim Crow, from Puerto Rican citizenship to *Hernández v. Texas* and beyond, racialized identities matter because the law will not loosen its grip on those it seeks to contain. Thinking otherwise, beyond the ecumenical standard, Sotomayor used "undocumented" and thereby infuriated conservatives by confirming their biases about the "wise Latina" mediapheme they inherited. Those who knew her previous record on the Second Circuit knew better. To some she was simply being a "Latina activist" by using the term "undocumented"; to others, she was making an invisible identity legible in a way that made the *doing,* but not the *being,* the link between the Latino subject and the reach of the law. In the process, she was making manifest the degree to which undocumented immigrants own their bodies and social identities in relation to the law.

Already earlier that year, in the *Citizens United v. Federal Elections Commission,* Sotomayor had joined four other justices in a dissent that questioned—among other things—the court majority's ruling that corporations are entitled to political speech and full First Amendment protections.[8] This signal case decided in 2010 found that corporations have a First Amendment right to expressly support political candidates for Congress and the White House. In his dissent, Justice John Paul Stevens noted a basic ecumenical principle regarding identity. "The basic premise underlying the court's ruling," he wrote, "is its iteration, and constant reiteration, of the proposition that the First Amendment *bars* regulatory distinctions based on a *speaker's identity*, including its *'identity'* as a corporation" (my emphasis). For Stevens, the Constitution prohibits, that is, it "bars," distinctions in treatment regarding "identities"; ergo, extending First Amendment protections to corporations violated established precedent. Not so, said the majority. The intricacies of the case are substantial and exceed my limits here, but it was the first high-profile case in which Sotomayor experienced both the thinking of her fellow colleagues and how the ecumenical standard as applied in constitutional thinking—an ostensibly "identity" free and colorblind Constitution—was constrained by the limits of its interpreters. That is, it demonstrated to her how even ecumenists invoke the social situatedness of "identity."

The following year, in *Michigan v. Bryant* (2011), Sotomayor authored her second majority opinion, in which we can see a clear shift in her juridical thinking from that of a Second Circuit "impartial" ecumenist to the otherwiseness that I have been describing.[9] The *Michigan v. Bryant* case involved a man, Anthony Covington, who after being shot drove himself to a gas station in Detroit, Michigan. Police found Covington bleeding on the ground at the station. As he lay dying, he told the police the identity of the man who shot him. Later, during a trial, the alleged shooter attempted to suppress the introduction of Covington's statements identifying him on the grounds that it was a violation of his Sixth Amendment right to confront his accuser. Writing for the majority, Sotomayor asserted that the lower court had made a mistake in considering Covington's last words "testimony" because the police officers were not conducting a formal interrogation but rather gathering required information to resolve what was an ongoing emergency. The temporality—Covington's *queer* timing—mattered here. In recognizing this, the court affirmed that a jury can hear a dying person's last words.

In the case, Scalia rejected Sotomayor's majority opinion in unusually caustic terms, even for him. He wrote of Sotomayor's opinion, "Today's tale—a story of five officers conducting successive examinations of a dying man with the primary purpose, not of obtaining and preserving his testimony regarding his killer, but of protecting him, them, and others from a murderer somewhere on the loose—is so transparently false that professing to believe it *demeans this institution*" (my emphasis). Scalia's dissent was scathing because he made no attempt at hiding the nature of the interpretive disagreement with Sotomayor over the Sixth Amendment. For Scalia, Sotomayor's legal reasoning in the case *was* precisely the problem. As such, for him it detracted meaning and purpose from the judiciary *as* an institution. For Scalia, Sotomayor's jurisprudential logic was so flawed that it wasn't worthy of the institution. In her response to Scalia's dissent, Sotomayor countered, "Unlike the dissent's apparent ability to read Covington's mind, we rely on the available evidence, which suggests that Covington perceived an ongoing threat." Following Sotomayor's otherwiseness, one might say that both context and the subjective position of the aggrieved mattered. For Scalia, Covington might have been an already dead subject in the eyes of the law, even before he died, but what mattered in the ruling was what the Supreme Court could interpret as "testimony." The case established the heft and direction of Sotomayor's thinking. Sonia Sotomayor was in the house.

The following year, in *National Federation of Independent Business v. Sebelius* (2012), otherwise known as the case that preserved the Affordable Care Act, Sotomayor voted to uphold congressional power to enact most provisions of the law that had been deridingly called "Obamacare." While this solidified the public perception of Sotomayor as a "liberal," it was conservative chief justice John Roberts who surprised both liberals and conservatives alike by siding with the premise of congressional power to uphold the law. It was not until the *Obergefell v. Hodges* (2015) decision that we would begin to understand the extent of Sotomayor's juridical thinking regarding "public accommodation laws." A landmark in civil rights jurisprudence, *Obergefell v. Hodges* is commonly referred to as the "marriage equality" case. In the case, the Supreme Court ruled that the fundamental right to marry is guaranteed to same-sex couples by both the Due Process Clause and the Equal Protection Clause of the Fourteenth Amendment.

During the *Obergefell* case hearings, Sotomayor questioned why the state could bar a class of people from equal treatment under the law. When she stated with aplomb during oral arguments that "the right to be married is embedded in the Constitution," ecumenists balked. Their logic was conveniently unencumbered by the history of anti-LGBTQ discrimination. The ecumenists' position was cynically simple: "Gays and lesbians can surely marry," went their argument. "They just need to marry someone of the opposite sex." That marriage itself guaranteed to straights more than a thousand legal protections that were denied to unmarried LGBTQ couples was of no consequence to these universalist ecumenists. After the 2015 *Obergefell v. Hodges* decision, conservative judicial activists directed their energies against LGBTQ equality by lobbying for the empty seat on Supreme Court left after Scalia's death in 2016. Trump's appointment of Christian conservative and Federalist Society member Neil Gorsuch to the court—in a seat that was kept unfilled for over a year because of Republican senator Mitch McConnell's obstructionism—provided just such an opportunity. *Masterpiece Cakeshop, Ltd. v. Colorado Civil Rights Commission* (2018) would provide just such a test case for conservative judicial activists.[10]

The case was a national headliner and centered on a Colorado baker, Jack Phillips, who refused to make a wedding cake for a gay male couple, David Mullins and Charlie Craig. Phillips held that making the cake for the couple conflicted with his religious beliefs. His lawyers, however, made the argument that his cakes were "art," thereby arguing that his refusal to accommodate Mullins and Craig constituted a form of free speech. If Phillips were compelled by the state to make the cake for the gay couple, they argued, the government would be infringing on his constitutionally protected First Amendment right to freedom of speech. The case was supported by the ironically named Alliance Defending Freedom (ADF), an American right-wing "Christian" nonprofit that focuses on legal advocacy in support of recriminalizing homosexuality in the United States and abroad (ADF's work abroad includes legal initiatives to sterilize transgender citizens).[11]

During oral arguments for the case, Sotomayor was tactically brilliant. She pointed out the absurdity of the central argument—cake *as* art—when she noted, "The primary purpose of a food of any kind is to be eaten.... Now, some people might love the aesthetic appeal of a special dessert, and look at it for a very long time, but in the end its only purpose is to be eaten." Phillips's lawyers were pigeonholed during oral arguments to claim that, in essence, the cakes were so expressive that they qualified as a form of speech. The ADF lawyers' arguments had to then center *not* on the "who" (a gay couple) but on "what" (cake as artistic expressions). In other words, refusing to serve gays was legal in this instance because it had to do not with discrimination of the person but with Phillips's "right" to free speech, uncompelled by the government. Focusing on juridical precedent, Sotomayor was clear about the nature of public accommodations law:

> We've always said in our public accommodations law we can't change your private beliefs. But if you want to be a part of our community, of our civic community, there's certain behavior, conduct [that] you can't engage in. And that includes not selling products that you sell to everyone else to people simply because of their race, religion, national origin, gender, and, in this case, sexual orientation.[12]

By doing so, Sotomayor made obvious the extent to which the ADF argument was precisely about discrimination, not freedom of expression. But with Gorsuch on the court, the writing was on the wall.

In the end the court's majority of legal originalists, all Federalist Society members, would support the ADF's agenda in favor of denying Mullins and Craig's public accommodation by upholding Phillips's claim that his cakes constituted a type of freedom of expression. At the close of oral arguments, and no doubt aware of how the decision would turn against Mullins and Craig, Sotomayor proffered a history lesson by drawing a stark parallel between gay marriage and interracial marriage. "The problem is that America's reaction to mixed marriages and to race didn't change on its own," she said. "It changed because we had public accommodation laws that forced people to do things that many claimed were against their expressive rights and against their religious rights." Sotomayor's exhortation not to forget the reach and purpose of public accommodation laws did not persuade either her newest colleague on the bench at the time or the other originalists. Gorsuch joined the extreme right on the court and in so doing affirmed that Phillips had a "free speech" right to discriminate against LGBTQ customers. This sharp split will likely mark how future cases will be interpreted by the court as the ADF and other similar right-wing alliances continue their assault on freedoms we thought protected by law. The ADF strategy in this case is telling nonetheless as we can now predict how the coming assault on public accommodation laws will center on "free speech." This will be especially significant in college and university settings where "free speech" initiatives will cloak the politically motivated intent of their backers: to erase out of existence the equity and inclusionary gains made by Black and Brown students, faculty, staff, and their allies, as well as the endangered knowledge projects that serve them *and* the democratic commons. As such, "otherwiseness" as an interpretive pragmatic frame for legal reasoning will require concerted attempts at countering the antidemocratic logics of organizations such as the ADF, and other far-right attempts to contain those bodies they wish to control through the reach of law. The irony is that the current mediapheme has it that the judicial branch, and Supreme Court in particular, has been "too liberal." Countering this alternative reality will require civil society participation that takes democratic participation and cause-effect relations seriously. Given the current composition of the court, it will be necessary to place greater focus on oral arguments moving forward as a way to both predict and delimit potentially dangerous interpretive positions as cases head to the Supreme Court. That such a strategy of containment is now necessary should alert us to how "court packing" by the extreme right has been largely successful at the expense of the democratic commons.

RACE MATTERS

Sotomayor's most significant legacy to date is related to education as a practice of freedom and how those freedoms stand to be diminished through inequitable access to the benefits of educational opportunities. As we saw earlier, the right-wing assault on educational opportunities for out-groups has been part of a broader concerted social-engineering agenda to delimit Black and Latino social mobility through the dismantling of legal protections that have attempted to level the playing field. In addition to rolling back LGBTQ protections through the agencies of the ADF, affirmative action has been the other primary battleground through which the extreme right have been engineering their antidemocratic social agenda on college and university campuses. Whereas ADF has provided the financial and legal support to roll back LGBTQ rights, the right-wing Students for Fair Admissions, also a designated nonprofit, has sought to challenge racial and ethnic classifications. Right-wing groups such as Students for Fair Admissions (SFFA), as well as the Project on Fair Representation (POFR), discussed in chapter 2, have attacked affirmative action to curtail civil rights and stymie racial equality. One of the most significant assaults on affirmative action was brought about through *Fisher v. University of Texas at Austin* (2013, 2016).[13] In *Fisher*, a white female applicant sued the university after being rejected for admission, arguing that the school's use of race violated the Equal Protection Clause of the Fourteenth Amendment. The case was initially brought to the court by POFR in 2013 and reached the court for a second time in 2016. In the second *Fisher* ruling, the court held that that universities may take race into account as long as that practice is narrowly tailored to avoid violating the Constitution's Equal Protection Clause. The antecedents to this 2016 decision merit commentary since doing so allows us to see how Sotomayor's thinking otherwise is providing a stopgap in the face of the continued erosion of what remains of affirmative action.

In *Schuette v. Coalition to Defend Affirmative Action* (2014), a 6–2 majority in the court upheld Michigan's ironically named Michigan Civil Rights Initiative. The case effectively delimited the use of race considerations in college admissions by ostensibly allowing a ban on race- and sex-based discrimination in Michigan's state constitution through the optic of "reverse racism."[14] Through the logic of "reverse racism," whites and men were being "discriminated" against when universities used "race" and "gender" selectively in assigning value to applicants in admissions decisions. In her dissent to the case, Sotomayor plainly stated, "The way to stop discrimination on the basis of race is to speak openly and candidly on the subject of race and to apply the Constitution with eyes open to the unfortunate effects of racial discrimination." The dissent, the first to be read by Sotomayor from the bench in her five years on the court, was also a rejoinder to Chief Justice Roberts's earlier plurality opinion in *Parents Involved v. Seattle School District No. 1* (2007). This earlier case overturned the Seattle public school system's use of race to improve diversity. In his majority opinion, Roberts had insisted on what amounted to a color-blind and, for many, seemingly ahistorical accounting of race in the country. "The way to stop discrimination on the basis of race is to stop discriminating on the basis of race," opined Roberts in 2007.[15] Roberts's majority opinion blindly conflated affirmative action policies to remedy legally sanctioned racism in the present with the likes of segregated lunch counters before the civil rights era. In *Schuette v. Coalition to Defend Affirmative Action* the majority opinion also held that "we should leave race out of the picture entirely and let the voters sort it out."

Refusing the Supreme Court's historical whitewashing, Sotomayor's dissent demonstrated the strongest indictment to date from a sitting Supreme Court justice of the nation's current state of "racism without racists." In her fifty-eight-page dissent, Sotomayor laid the groundwork for the scaffolding that would belie the purportedly color-blind ecumenical standard used by the likes of POFR and SFFA and extended by Chief Justice Roberts himself. The scaffolding provided by Sotomayor has created a roadmap for future judicial thinking. She wrote, "Race matters. Race matters in part because of the long history of racial minorities' being denied access to the political process," she explained. "Race also matters because of persistent racial inequality in society—inequality that cannot be ignored and that has produced stark socioeconomic disparities." In the dissent, Sotomayor inscribed Black and Brown affect as the basis on which to understand race through otherwiseness:

> And race matters for reasons that really are only skin deep, that cannot be discussed any other way, and that cannot be wished away. Race matters to a young man's view of society when he spends his teenage years watching others tense up as he passes, no matter the neighborhood where he grew up. Race matters to a young woman's sense of self when she states her hometown, and then is pressed, "No, where are you really from?", regardless of how many generations her family has been in the country. Race matters to a young person addressed by a stranger in a foreign language, which he does not understand because only English was spoken at home. Race matters because of the slights, the snickers, the silent judgments that reinforce that most crippling of thoughts: "I do not belong here."[16]

Sotomayor's strident dissent in the *Schuette* case evinces most clearly what I am here calling the emergence of Latino legal thought insofar as she made race a phenomenological consideration in jurisprudential thinking. When others "tense up" as you pass them, when a citizen is always already an outsider—"No, where are you really from?"—when your way of experiencing the world is always already circumscribed by your outsider status as understood by majority culture, then you are not protected by laws in quite the same way as those whom the law has always served. Sotomayor offered evidence in her dissent that explained how the end of affirmative action in California in 1996 with the passage of Proposition 209 had, as *Schuette* would, bring a steep decline in Latino and Black enrollment. In so doing, Sotomayor's otherwiseness characterized Michigan's affirmative action ban as another instance in which the majority "votes" to enact legislation that harms minorities.

It is not a stretch to concede that Sotomayor's reasoning, as evidenced in her 2014 *Schuette* dissent, provided the necessary groundwork for countering the second arrival of *Fisher* to the court in 2016. As I previously noted, the Supreme Court reaffirmed in 2016 that universities can take race into account to ensure a diverse student body as long as that practice is narrowly tailored to avoid violating the Equal Protection Clause. As of this writing, SFFA has filed suit against Harvard University, claiming that its affirmative action policies violated the Equal Protection Clause. While the lower court has dismissed the group's argument, it is predicted that the case will reach the Supreme Court. With Kavanaugh and Gorsuch now installed on the court, we would do well to brace for what is coming as the unrelenting assault on what's left of affirmative action continues.

As I have shown, Sotomayor's trajectory from "ecumenical universalist" to the otherwiseness that Muñoz has described as the feeling of "being Brown," an affective phenomenological way of knowing, is instructive of the degree to which ethnic

subjects can aspire to a seat at the proverbial table, the democratic commons, or the court. The emergence of Latino legal
thought should alert us to both the promise and the limits of
political enfranchisement through law. The inevitable demise of
what remains of affirmative action on the horizon stands to create the groundswell that democratic practice demands as the
"sleeping giant" of electoral politics awakens to find itself at
either the table of democratic enfranchisement or the edge of
democracy's graveyard. What is clear is that confounding symbolic representation with political enfranchisement proper
comes with a heavy price. It is a price, a type of knowing, that
Sotomayor may have learned in the nick of time and one that we
would do well to account for as Latinos and as Americans.

CONCLUSION: SELF-EXPRESSION AS FASCISM

> Fascism sees its salvation in giving [the] masses not
> their right, but instead a chance to express
> themselves. The masses have a right to change
> property relations; Fascism seeks to give them an
> expression while preserving property.
> Walter Benjamin[17]

Walter Benjamin discusses the "aestheticization" of politics in his
1936 essay "The Work of Art in the Age of Its Technological
Reproduction." For Benjamin, the right to "self-expression" without political power *is* fascism. When he says that the masses have
a right to property relations, he means to say that people have a
right to both corporeal and intellectual autonomy, a right to be
free from subjection because they aren't the property of the state
and are free to act on their own free will. While there is no evidence that I am aware of that Benjamin was versed in the intricacies of American law or political culture, it does not belie the fact

that the history of people *as* "property" is astounding in that it was only made manifest through law in human history in the United States. This is because the United States is the only nation-state to make slavery a permanent condition of *being* in and through law, and the U.S. Civil War was perhaps the most painful corrective to the democratic recognition of that injustice.

Benjamin was, as were the slaveholding forefathers who drafted the U.S. Constitution, well versed in Enlightenment thought, and was no doubt aware of Locke's dictum "Lives, liberties and estates are our property because we own our bodies." Locke's "labor theory" of property established the nature of property claims in post-Enlightenment reasoning and jurisprudence. For Locke, the apple belongs to you if you picked it, as does the basket for carrying them because you created it. Unless of course you are a slaveholding forefather, in which case you ensure that you count Blacks as three-fifths of a person and enshrine said belief in the U.S. Constitution.[18]

Benjamin, writing in 1936, was prescient in identifying how fascism treats the category of "the political" simply as a spectacle, and in the process, he later avers, you become the object of the spectacle once you give to another your right to autonomy of body and thought. Without considering such consequences, a disaffected but comfortable-enough populace, interested only in preserving what it understands as its class-specific self-expressive interests, stands to be seduced by the possibilities and satisfactions accorded to self-expression at the expense of the political clout that would make such expression meaningful through self-governance. Benjamin was simply reminding his readers that in the *res publica* you are a politically dead subject when you confound expressive culture with the politics of the state. Facebook fake news, anyone? Be forewarned. Understanding this in our current political culture is necessary in order to counter the current national pedagogies that attempt to lure us into an apprenticeship in the cult of power *as* cruelty through media spectacles devoid of ethical accountability. This unethical turn demeans our ability to distinguish truth from fiction, cost from value, and exalts the brutal expediency of absolute power above righteousness. In the end, the rewards of recognizing the importance of the political over the expressive, of real political representation over symbolic representation, will provide either egalitarian satisfaction, limited dividends, or even simply disillusionment. It will all depend on where we stand, and what we stand to lose, in the democratic commons. I believe that ultimately it is in the act of resisting the siren call of expressive affiliation, by demanding political self-possession *as* self-determination, that we can begin to creatively answer democracy's clarion call for just governance in order to make demagoguery the provenance of the bread and circuses of yore. It is time to practice self-governance and the arts of determined self-possession as a positive freedom, not as the solipsistic negative freedom to retreat from the democratic commons. The moment is now, and the rewards will be ours, in and beyond the democratic Brown commons, if we get it right.

ACKNOWLEDGMENTS

I have carried the weight of this book with guarded optimism since Sonia Sotomayor's confirmation to the Supreme Court in 2009. But then I read Lauren Berlant's *Cruel Optimism* (2011), and my own optimism, guarded though it was, was no more. I am not publicly blaming Lauren for my disillusionment here. I am instead thanking her for the theoretical vocabulary with which to apprehend our historical moment's primary lesson in affective and political disaffection. "Optimism," she averred, "is cruel when the object/scene that ignites a sense of possibility actually makes it impossible to attain the expansive transformation for which a person or a people risks a striving." The nearly completed book that I had carried went to the wayside—as did much of my affective striving—and instead I wrote *Being Brown*. I did so because the enabling fictions of political enfranchisement that emerged, particularly after the reelection of Barack Obama, were too neatly premised on the "hope" of a future fulfillment that for Latinos, as for Godot, never quite arrived in any structurally meaningful way despite the striving. The recognition has made me a bit of a political killjoy, but as Paulo Freire reminded us, *conscientização*, critical consciousness, comes at a price, but the value of the awakening brings us closer to practices of freedom. I have incurred many debts in the process, and I take pleasure in acknowledging them here.

Niels Hooper, executive editor at the University of California Press, and Robin Manley, along with American Studies Now series editors Lisa Duggan and Curtis Marez, made *Being Brown* possible, and I am grateful for their fine stewardship. Thanks are due to Kate Hoffman and Pablo Morales for shepherding the book through its final stages. I am also indebted to the anonymous reviewers whose suggestions have made this a better book. Early on, Chris Cunningham helped channel the current incarnation of this project in the right direction. I thank him for his instincts, fashion sense, and the friendship that we sealed after we met as graduate students at a party in Jack Halberstam's San Diego loft many moons ago through the agencies of Daniel Contreras. During that exceptionally raucous and, frankly, legendary Modern Language Association party, I also met many of my now old friends, as well as the intellectual mainstays who have accompanied me since, including Ricardo Ortiz and the late José Esteban Muñoz, not to mention the host extraordinaire.

I received many opportunities to refine my thinking and learn from colleagues who invited me to present versions of *Being Brown*. Claudia Milian's intellectual generosity provided the initial impetus for the project, and it gives me great pleasure to acknowledge her here. I am deeply grateful to the following for either the invitations, encouragement, support, or all of the above: Billy Acree, Matt Armstead, Cristina Beltrán, Ana Brickhouse, Carolyn Brown, Israel Burshatin, Raúl Coronado, Arlene Dávila, Arcadio Díaz-Quiñones, Elena Gorfinkel, Carmen Lamas, Carla Marcoantonio, Juliana Martínez, Yolanda Martínez-San Miguel, Nancy Raquel Mirabal, Ricardo Ortiz, Christopher Pérez, Cat Ramírez, Israel Reyes, John Río Riofrio, Wadda Ríos-Font, Juana María Rodríguez, Nicolás Shumway, Mary Sias, Kirsten Silva Gruesz, José Quiroga, and Salvador Vidal-Ortiz, among many others, stand out for special mention. José Esteban Muñoz passed away before we could compare the wise Latina stories we promised to share at a future American Studies Association panel. That his work still illuminates the way forward, back, around, across, and beyond, for so many, continues to provide solace.

Many colleagues and friends at the University of Richmond have created the conditions that allow exceptional teacher-scholars and intellectually committed students to thrive. While I can't thank them all here, I would be remiss not to mention Paul Achter, Jannette Amaral-Rodríguez, Laura Browder, Erika Damer, Alicia Díaz, Miguel Díaz-Barriga, Margret Dorsey, Rubí Escalona, Sharon Feldman, Libby Grunner, Patricia Herrera, Crystal Hoyt, Lucretia McCulley, Del McWhorter, Mariela Méndez, Mari Lee Misfud, Ángel Otero-Blanco, Sara Pappas, Lidia Radi, Patrice Rankine, Bedelia Richards, Julietta Singh, Andrea Simpson, Kathleen Skerrett, Nathan Snaza, Rania Sweiss, and Allison Tait. I especially thank Sara and Chris Pappas for the sage counsel that arrived in the nick of time. My new colleagues at Hunter College, CUNY, have made my return to my alma mater gratifying, and Anthony P. Browne and Arlene Torres stand out for special mention.

I also wish to thank the dedicated librarians and staff at the following institutions for facilitating access to their special collections and providing research support: the Beinecke Rare Book and Manuscript Library at Yale University; the José M. Lázaro Library at the University of Puerto Rico, Río Piedras; the Manuscripts, Archives and Rare Books Division of the Schomburg Center for Research in Black Culture of the New York Public Library; the Archives of the Puerto Rican Diaspora, Centro de Estudios Puertorriqueños, Hunter College, CUNY; the Firestone Library at Princeton University; the National Museum of the U.S. Navy in Washington, DC; and the National Archives and Records Administration in College Park, Maryland. Additionally, a research fellowship at American University's Center for Latin American and Latino Studies allowed me to complete this book. I thank CLALS director Eric Hershberg for the opportunity, support, and connections he facilitated.

The broader community of academics, activists, and affective constants I've found in DC since graduate school keeps reminding me that chosen family is a gift. Ricardo Ortiz's brilliance is already legendary, but it is his support of Latino studies and students that makes his broader work so essential, especially in the capital city at this historical juncture, and I'm grateful to him for his example. Nancy Raquel Mirabal's intelligence and wisdom have been essential to building Latino community since her arrival in DC, and the capital city is better for it. As I closed one door, the incomparable Rob Falk opened another. I'm indebted to him for this and for the friendship we've fostered over two decades. I'm also lucky to count on a crew of exceptional stalwarts who help bridge the distance between my DC and New York City chosen families without too much wear and tear: Bobby Alexander, Eric Bartheld, Jason Hall, Paul Kelleher, Daniel Neep, and Eliza Reshefsky have all made it possible to run away from chthonian drudgery when I've needed it most. I'm better for their company, provisions, and the Dionysian escapes that make it impossible for me to refuse.

My family in both Connecticut and Cuba's northernmost city—also known as Miami—continue to put up with me. They still somehow know what I need to feel most at home, and I consider myself fortunate for that anchor. Osi Gutiérrez and Lisette León, *primos hermanos extraordinarios,* continue to inspire me with the generosity of heart and spirit I'm still perfecting. This book is dedicated to Christina Valera, and to Liska and Alex Gutiérrez, *divinos tesoros.* They may not know it yet, but they are creating the way out of the cruel optimism of the day through their audacious insistence on being Brown outside the strictures that would contain them. Acknowledging this doesn't make me a hopeful closet optimist, just a proud forerunner in a much longer journey toward what I've here called the Brown democratic commons.

NOTES

INTRODUCTION

1. Sonia Sotomayor, *My Beloved World* (New York: Alfred A. Knopf, 2013), 178.

2. Sotomayor consistently refers to herself as a "Latina," and I respect that preference in this book. Consequently, I will follow standard Spanish usage for the demonym *Latino*. Both the masculine *Latino* and feminine *Latina* can be used as adjectives as well as nouns. The singular masculine form *Latino,* however, can function as a generic noun to refer to both men and women. While the plural noun *Latinas* refers to more than one female, the plural *Latinos* refers to either a group of males or to a group of both males and females.

3. The majority of the 57.5 million Latinos in the United States are native born, while approximately 19.6 million are immigrants. The population of Latino immigrants comprises various juridical designations, including "lawful permanent residents," "conditional permanent residents," "temporary visitors" (who include students with F-1 visas, business visitors or tourists on B1 or B2 visas, and K-1 visa holders), "asylum seekers," and "undocumented immigrants." For a review and breakdown of these categories, see the United States Census Bureau, "The Hispanic Population in the United States: 2016," last updated

August 29, 2018, https://www.census.gov/data/tables/2016/demo /hispanic-origin/2016-cps.html. See also Gustavo López, Kristen Bialik, and Jynnah Radford, "Key Findings about U.S. Immigrants," Pew Research Center, November 30, 2018, http://www.pewresearch.org /fact-tank/2018/11/30/key-findings-about-u-s-immigrants/.

4. After the U.S.-Mexico War (1846–48), the United States conquered Mexico's northern territories, including modern-day Arizona, California, Nevada, and Utah; parts of Colorado, New Mexico, Oklahoma, and Wyoming; and Mexico's territorial claims in Texas, which had been under U.S. occupation since 1836 (the Gadsden Purchase of 1853 further extended Arizona's and New Mexico's territorial lines into Mexico). The annexation of Mexican territories, however, tells only part of the story. With the incorporation of former Spanish dominions such as modern-day Florida and parts of the Gulf of Mexico region, we are left with a historical lacuna that yet has to be fully accounted for.

5. Political scientists refer to the phenomenon of representative personhood as "symbolic representation." The classic text on symbolic representation is Hanna Fenichel Pitkin's *The Concept of Representation* (Berkeley: University of California Press, 1967).

6. José Esteban Muñoz, "Wise Latinas," *Criticism* 56, no. 2 (2014), https://digitalcommons.wayne.edu/criticism/vol56/iss2/6.

7. José Esteban Muñoz, "Feeling Brown, Feeling Down: Latina Affect, the Performativity of Race, and the Depressive Position," *Signs* 31, no. 3 (Spring 2006): 675–88.

8. Barbara Ransby, *Making All Black Lives Matter: Reimagining Freedom in the 21st Century* (Berkeley: University of California Press, 2018).

9. A fragment from *Sense of Brown,* "Preface: Fragment from the *Sense of Brown* Manuscript," appeared in Nadja Millner-Larsen and Gavin Butt's "The Queer Commons," *GLQ* 24, no. 4 (2018): 395–97. Muñoz's *Sense of Brown* is being edited for publication by Joshua Chambers-Letson and Tavia Nyong'o. Claudia Milian offers an important critique of the epistemologies of "Brown" in *Latining America: Black-Brown Passages and the Coloring of Latino/a Studies* (Athens: University of Georgia Press, 2013).

10. Tavia Nyong'o, "Barack Hussein Obama, or, The Name of the Father," *Scholar and Feminist Online*, no. 7.2 (Spring 2009), http://sfonline.barnard.edu/africana/nyongo_01.htm.

CHAPTER ONE. SONIA SOTOMAYOR AND "THE LATINO QUESTION"

1. W.E.B. Du Bois, *The Souls of Black Folk*, ed. Brent Hayes Edwards (New York: Oxford University Press, 2007 [1903]), 7.

2. Leo R. Chávez, *The Latino Threat: Constructing Immigrants, Citizens, and the Nation*, 2nd ed. (Stanford, CA: Stanford University Press, 2013 [2008]), iv.

3. Imani Perry, *More Beautiful and More Terrible: The Embrace and Transcendence of Racial Inequality in the United States* (New York: NYU Press, 2011), 52.

4. Ira Katznelson, *When Affirmative Action Was White: An Untold History of Racial Inequality in Twentieth-Century America* (New York: W.W. Norton, 2005), 175.

5. James McKinley Jr., "Texas Conservatives Win Curriculum Change," *New York Times*, March 12, 2010, http://www.nytimes.com/2010/03/13/education/13texas.html; Manny Fernández and Christine Hauser, "Texas Mother Teaches Textbook Company a Lesson on Accuracy," *New York Times*, October 6, 2015; Laura Isensee, "Why Calling Slaves 'Workers' Is More Than an Editing Error," NPR, October 23, 2015, https://www.npr.org/sections/ed/2015/10/23/450826208/why-calling-slaves-workers-is-more-than-an-editing-error.

6. Dana Chivvis, "Arizona Outlaws Mexican-American Studies Program," *AOL News/Huffington Post*, January 10, 2011, http://www.aolnews.com/2011/01/10/arizona-outlaws-mexican-american-studies-program/.

7. Rafia Zakaria, "How Trump Is Stripping Immigrants of Their Citizenship," *Nation*, December 21, 2018, https://www.thenation.com/article/denaturalization-trump-citizenship-emma-goldman/.

8. Schneider v. Rusk, 377 U.S. 163 (1964), https://supreme.justia.com/cases/federal/us/377/163/.

9. Dara Lind, "Trump's Stripping of Passports from Some Texas Latinos, Explained," *Vox,* August 30, 2018, https://www.vox.com/2018/8/30/17800410/trump-passport-birth-certificate-hispanic-denial-citizens.

10. Eoin Higgins, "How ICE Works to Strip Citizenship from Naturalized Americans," *Intercept,* February 14, 2018, https://theintercept.com/2018/02/14/ice-denaturalization-naturalized-citizen-immigration/.

11. Jean Stefancic and Richard Delgado, *No Mercy: How Conservative Think Tanks and Foundations Changed America's Social Agenda* (Philadelphia: Temple University Press, 1996).

12. Ibid., 155.

13. Jason Richwine, "IQ and Immigration Policy" (PhD diss., Harvard University, 2009), 63.

14. The number of native-born Latinos in 2009 was at just over 62 percent. Data on immigrant versus native-born Latinos would have been easily available to Richwine, including data from the Census Bureau. That percentage remains steady today at just over 63 percent.

15. For a discussion of the Great Society as the most significant attempt at national reform since President Franklin Delano Roosevelt's New Deal, see John A. Andrew III, *Lyndon Johnson and the Great Society* (Lanham, MD: Rowman and Littlefield, 1998).

16. Michael P. Jefferies, *Paint the White House Black: Barack Obama and the Meaning of Race in America* (Palo Alto, CA: Stanford University Press, 2013), 4.

17. Jason Richwine, "Are Liberals Smarter than Conservatives?," *American,* October 21, 2009, http://www.aei.org/publication/are-liberals-smarter-than-conservatives/. Richwine was referencing Harvard law professor Larry Tribe's leaked memo to President Obama warning that Sotomayor "is not nearly as smart as she seems to think she is." Al Kamen, "Laurence Tribe Unfiltered on Sonia Sotomayor," *Washington Post,* October 28, 2010, http://voices.washingtonpost.com/44/2010/10/laurence-tribe-unfiltered-on-s.html. Tribe eventually conceded that he was wrong about Sotomayor and that she had become a formidable associate justice of the Supreme Court.

18. Laura Reston, "Where Trump Gets His Fuzzy Border Math: Meet the Far-Right 'Think Tank' Working to Legitimize the Immi-

gration Crackdown," *New Republic,* March 10, 2017, https://newrepublic.com/article/140951/trump-gets-fuzzy-border-math.

19. Charles Murray, "In Defense of Jason Richwine," *National Review,* May 15, 2013, http://www.nationalreview.com/article/348323/defense-jason-richwine. In his dissertation, Richwine acknowledged his debt to Murray: "no one has been more influential." Richwine, "IQ and Immigration Policy," v.

20. Anita Merina et al., "What's Her Number? Zip Codes Tell Us a Lot about Public School Quality," *NEA Today,* August 22, 2013, http://neatoday.org/2013/08/22/whats-her-number-zip-codes-tell-us-a-lot-about-public-school-quality/.

21. Robert Rector and Jason Richwine noted,

> If amnesty is enacted, the average adult unlawful immigrant would receive $592,000 more in government benefits over the course of his remaining lifetime than he would pay in taxes. Over a lifetime, the former unlawful immigrants together would receive $9.4 trillion in government benefits and services and pay $3.1 trillion in taxes. They would generate a lifetime fiscal deficit (total benefits minus total taxes) of $6.3 trillion. (All figures are in constant 2010 dollars.) This should be considered a minimum estimate.

See their "The Fiscal Cost of Unlawful Immigrants and Amnesty to the U.S. Taxpayer," Heritage Foundation, May 6, 2013, https://www.heritage.org/immigration/report/the-fiscal-cost-unlawful-immigrants-and-amnesty-the-us-taxpayer.

22. Callum Patton, "Trump Wall: Israeli Company to Make Prototype for His Mexico Border Wall," *Newsweek,* September 14, 2017, http://www.newsweek.com/trump-wall-israeli-company-make-prototype-200000-mile-long-mexico-border-wall-664968; Associated Press, "Prototypes for Trump's Wall, including Israeli Model, Take Shape on Border," *Times of Israel,* October 20, 2017, https://www.timesofisrael.com/prototypes-for-trumps-wall-including-israeli-model-take-shape-on-border/.

23. Eduardo Bonilla-Silva, *Racism without Racists: Color-Blind Racism and the Persistence of Racial Inequality in America* (Lanham, MD: Rowman and Littlefield, 2013).

24. Ibid., 3–4.

25. Bias against Sotomayor's nomination was not just the provenance of conservative commentators. The most significant attack against Sotomayor appeared in the *New Republic*. According to the magazine's legal affairs editor, Jeffrey Rosen, there was no evidence that she was "a judicial star of the highest intellectual caliber." "The Case against Sotomayor," May, 4 2009, http://www.newrepublic.com /article/politics/the-case-against-sotomayor.

26. Mendez v. Westminister School Dist., 64 F. Supp. 544 (S.D. Cal. 1946), https://law.justia.com/cases/federal/district-courts/FSupp/64/544 /1952972/.

27. Joshua Chambers-Letson, "Embodying Justice: The Making of Justice Sonia Sotomayor," *Women and Performance: A Journal of Feminist Theory* 20, no. 2 (July 2010): 149–72.

28. Hernandez v. Texas, 347 U.S. 475 (1954), https://supreme.justia .com/cases/federal/us/347/475/.

29. Michael A. Olivas, *Colored Men and Hombres Aquí: Hernández v. Texas and the Emergence of Mexican American Lawyering* (Houston: Arte Público Press, 2006), 218.

30. Lázaro Lima, "Negotiating Cultural Memory in the Aftermath of the Mexican-American War: Nineteenth Century Testimonials and *The Squatter and the Don*," chap. 1. in *The Latino Body: Crisis Identities in American Literary and Cultural Memory* (New York: NYU Press, 2007).

31. For a summative analysis of Operation Wetback, see Neil Foley, *Mexicans in the Making of America* (Cambridge, MA: Belknap Press of Harvard University Press, 2014), 123–47.

CHAPTER TWO. SONIA SOTOMAYOR'S ELUSIVE EMBRACE

1. Suzanne Mettler, *Degrees of Inequality: How the Politics of Higher Education Sabotaged the American Dream* (New York: Basic Books, 2014), 38–39.

2. National Education Association, "High School Attendance, Graduation, Completion, and Dropout Statistics," last updated May 2018, https://nces.ed.gov/programs/coe/indicator_coi.asp.

3. Frances Negrón-Muntaner was one of the few commentators to thoughtfully critique the limits of this rebranded form of nationalism, and my work is indebted to her for having done so. See her "Confirmed: Sonia Sotomayor and the Limits of Latino Political Incorporation," *Journal of Transnational American Studies* 3, no. 2 (2011), https://escholarship.org/uc/item/4nb9249f.

4. Sotomayor's memoir remained on the *New York Times* nonfiction best-seller list for half the year, including four weeks in the number one spot.

5. Jodi Kantor, "Sotomayor, a Star on the Book-Tour Circuit, Sees a New Niche for a Justice," *New York Times,* February 3, 2013.

6. Ibid.

7. Hedrick Smith, *Who Stole the American Dream?* (New York: Random House, 2012), xvi.

8. Ibid., 71.

9. Jennifer L. Hochschild, *The American Dream and the Public Schools* (New York: Oxford University Press, 2003), 10.

10. Sandra Lilley, "Poll: 1 out of 3 Americans Inaccurately Think Most Hispanics Are Undocumented," NBC Latino, September 9, 2012, http://nbclatino.com/2012/09/12/poll-1-out-of-3-americans-think-most-hispanics-are-undocumented/.

11. For an account of the origins of "Latinos" in the United States, see my "Spanish Speakers and Early Latino Expression," in *American History through Literature, 1820–1870,* vol. 3, ed. Janet Gabler-Hover and Robert Sattelmeyer (New York: Charles Scribner's, 2006), 1118–23.

12. For high school graduation and dropout rates, see the National Center for Education Statistics, *Trends in High School Dropout and Completion Rates in the United States: 1972–2009, Compendium Report,* October 2011, http://nces.ed.gov/pubs2012/2012006.pdf. For Latino college enrollment and graduation rates, see Richard Fry, "Hispanic College Enrollment Spikes, Narrowing Gaps with Other Groups," Pew Research Hispanic Center, August 25, 2011, http://www.pewhispanic.org/2011/08/25/hispanic-college-enrollment-spikes-narrowing-gaps-with-other-groups/.

13. Buffy Smith, *Mentoring At-Risk Students through the Hidden Curriculum of Higher Education* (Lanham, MD: Lexington Books, 2013), xii.

14. Rebecca Diamond, "U.S. Workers' Diverging Locations: Policy and Inequality Implications," *SIEPR Policy Brief,* July 2014, https://siepr.stanford.edu/sites/default/files/publications/PolicyBrief-7-14-Diamond_0_2.pdf.

15. Sotomayor, *My Beloved World,* 191.

16. Ibid.

17. Michael R. Botson Jr., "No Gold Watch for Jima Crow's Retirement," in *Texas Labor History,* ed. Bruce A. Glasrud and James C. Maroney (College Station, TX: Texas A&M University Press, 2013), 348–49.

18. Robert Fullinwider, "Affirmative Action," in *Stanford Encyclopedia of Philosophy* (Fall 2013 edition), ed. Edward N. Zalta, last updated September 17, 2013, http://plato.stanford.edu/archives/fall2013/entries/affirmative-action/.

19. Sotomayor, *My Beloved World,* 188–89. In 2005 the firm merged into Pillsbury, Winthrop, Shaw, Pittman, LLP. Martin Krall is still practicing in its Washington, DC, office as senior counsel.

20. Reporters James Oliphant and Andrew Zajac cold-called Krall and his firm for comment. After reaching Krall in his vacation home in Florida, he said, "I've got nothing to say. That was 30 years ago." The law firm issued a statement: "Pillsbury is committed to diversity of all kinds, and we are proud of our record in attracting and retaining minority lawyers. Having attorneys from diverse backgrounds and experiences is fundamental to our business." See Oliphant and Zajac's "At Yale, Sotomayor Won Apology from Law Firm," *Los Angeles Times,* May 28, 2009, http://articles.latimes.com/2009/may/28/nation/na-sotomayor-apology28.

21. Regents of Univ. of California v. Bakke, 438 U.S. 265 (1978), https://supreme.justia.com/cases/federal/us/438/265/.

22. Evelyn Hu-DeHart, "Affirmative Action, Civil Rights, and Racial Preferences in the U.S.: Some General Observations," in *Affirmative Action in China and the U.S.: A Dialogue on Inequality and Minority Education,* ed. Minglang Zhou and Ann Maxell Hill (New York: Palgrave Macmillan, 2010), 220.

23. Christopher Newfield, *Unmaking the Public University: The Forty-Year Assault on the Middle Class* (Cambridge, MA: Harvard University Press, 2008), 111.

24. Ibid., 112.

25. Ibid., 113.

26. Martha Minow, Richard A. Shweder, and Hazel Rose Markus, "Pursuing Equal Education in Societies of Difference," in *Just Schools: Pursuing Equality in Societies of Difference,* ed. Martha Minow, Richard A. Shweder, and Hazel Rose Markus (New York: Russell Sage Foundation, 2008), 10.

27. Education studies scholars James A. Banks and Cherry A. McGee Banks summarize the definition of multiculturalism that I follow here: "a philosophical position and movement that assumes that the gender, ethnic, racial, and cultural diversity of pluralistic society should be reflected in all of the institutionalized structures of educational institutions." See their *Multicultural Education: Issues and Perspectives* (New York: Wiley, 2009), 474.

28. Exit polls showed that 77 percent of Latinos voted against Prop 187. For an analysis, see Pilar Marrero, *Killing the American Dream: How Anti-immigration Extremists Are Destroying the Nation* (New York: Palgrave Macmillan, 2012), 29–33.

29. Michigan passed a similar amendment in 2006 known as the Michigan Civil Rights Initiative, which followed California's lead and further eviscerated affirmative action's standing on a national scale as a largely successful program for enfranchising underrepresented minorities.

30. Lani Guinier and Gerald Torres, *The Miner's Canary: Enlisting Race, Resisting Power, Transforming Democracy* (Cambridge, MA: Harvard University Press, 2003), 277.

31. POFR is affiliated with the right-wing Project Liberty, a nonprofit that describes itself as "public charity whose mission is to support litigation that challenges racial and ethnic classifications." The group was behind the 2013 *Fisher vs. University of Texas at Austin* case. The first recruiting website for POFR to launch was directed to students rejected from the University of Wisconsin, Madison. The Fisher redux case, known as *Fisher II,* reached SCOTUS in 2016 and is discussed in the coda.

32. Madeline Masucci and Lynn Langton, *Hate Crime Victimization, 2004–2015,* special report, NCJ 250653 (Washington, DC: Bureau of

Justice Statistics, U.S. Department of Justice), 6, https://www.bjs.gov/content/pub/pdf/hcv0415.pdf. Frances Negrón-Muntaner et al. have qualified the nature and extent of hate crimes against Latinos in *The Latino Media Gap: A Report on the State of Latinos in the U.S. Media* (New York: Columbia University Center for the Study of Ethnicity and Race, 2014), 30–34. The full report can be found here: https://docs.wixstatic.com/ugd/73fa65_e8b1b4ec675c41b3a06f351926129cea.pdf.

33. Sumi Cho, "Post-racialism," *Iowa Law Review* 94 (2009): 1589–649.

34. Vijay Prashad, *Uncle Swami: South Asians in America Today* (New York: New Press, 2012), 101–2.

35. *Los Angeles Times,* "Full Text of Barack Obama 4th News Conference: Iran and Healthcare," June 23, 2009, http://latimesblogs.latimes.com/washington/2009/06/barack-obama-news-conference-transcript.html.

36. Bonilla-Silva, *Racism without Racists,* 4.

37. Tim Wise, *Colorblind: The Rise of Post-racial Politics and the Retreat from Racial Equity* (San Francisco: City Lights, 2010), 20.

38. Associated Press, "More Blacks, Latinos in Jail than College Dorms: Civil Rights Advocates Say Census Bureau Figures Are Startling," NBC, September 27, 2007, http://www.nbcnews.com/id/21001543/ns/us_news-life/t/more-Blacks-latinos-jail-college-dorms/#.UeW-8eRbV5bw. See also Devah Pager, "The Mark of a Criminal Record," *American Journal of Sociology* 108 (2003): 957–60; Devah Pager, Bruce Western, and Bart Bonikowski, "Discrimination in a Low Wage Labor Market: A Field Experiment," *American Sociological Review* 74 (October 2009): 777–79.

39. Patricia Gándara and Frances Contreras, *The Latino Education Crisis: The Consequences of Failed Social Policies* (Cambridge, MA: Harvard University Press, 2009), 1–2.

40. Ibid., 2.

41. Ibid., 305.

42. Anthony P. Carnevale and Jeff Strohl, *Separate and Unequal: How Higher Education Reinforces the Intergenerational Reproduction of White Racial Privilege* (Washington, DC: Georgetown Public Policy Institute, 2013), http://cew.georgetown.edu/separateandunequal/.

43. Ibid., 29.

CHAPTER THREE. SONIA SOTOMAYOR, THE MEDIAPHEME

1. MSNBC, "Obama Introduces Sonia Sotomayor as His Nominee for Supreme Court," YouTube video, 11:25, May 2, 2009, https://www.youtube.com/watch?v=GqShO72gQq4. For the complete transcript, see CNN, "Transcript of Obama-Sotomayor Announcement," last updated May 26, 2009, http://www.cnn.com/2009/POLITICS/05/26/obama.sotomayor.transcript/index.html.

2. David Maraniss's biography *Barack Obama: The Story* (2012) went on to raise questions about the president's characterization of his own life in *Dreams of My Father*. Maraniss noted that Obama's inaccuracies in his memoir and emphasis on his rags-to-riches story told through "a racial lens" merely reflected "pressures to try to tell a story" familiar to Americans.

3. *Democracy Now!*, "Confirmation Hearings Open for Judge Sonia Sotomayor, First Latina Nominated to Supreme Court," July 14, 2009, https://www.democracynow.org/2009/7/14/confirmation_hearings_begin_for_judge_sonia.

4. The same year, Justice Antonin Scalia earned almost $64,000 in royalties for his academic book *Reading Law: The Interpretation of Legal Texts*. All figures are reported by the justices in yearly financial disclosures. Bill Mears, "Sotomayor's Life Story Is Lucrative," *Political Ticker* (blog), CNN, June, 7 2013, http://politicalticker.blogs.cnn.com/2013/06/07/sotomayors-life-story-is-lucrative/.

5. Kenneth W. Mack, *Representing the Race: The Creation of the Civil Rights Lawyer* (Cambridge, MA: Harvard University Press, 2012), 4.

6. S. Paige Baty coins the term in *American Monroe: The Making of a Body Politic* (Berkeley: University of California Press, 1995), 60.

7. Kenneth W. Mack, *Representing the Race: The Creation of the Civil Rights Lawyer* (Cambridge, MA: Harvard University Press, 2012), 37.

8. Sotomayor's Judge Mario G. Olmos Memorial Lecture, "A Latina Judge's Voice," was published in the Spring 2002 issue of *La Raza Law Journal* and reproduced on the *New York Times* website, May 14, 2009, http://www.nytimes.com/2009/05/15/us/politics/15judge.text.html.

9. F. Michael Higginbothom, *Ghosts of Jim Crow: Ending Racism in Post-racial America* (New York: NYU Press, 2013), 20.

10. Stephanie Condon, "GOP Pushback Continues, with Limbaugh Calling Sotomayor a 'Reverse Racist,'" CBS News, May 27, 2009, https://www.cbsnews.com/news/gop-pushback-continues-with-limbaugh-calling-sotomayor-a-reverse-racist/.

11. Andy Martin, "Second Circuit Gossip: Sotomayor 'Deeply-Closeted' Lesbian/Cougar," *Contrarian Commentary,* June 1, 2009, https://contrariancommentary.wordpress.com/2009/06/01/second-circuit-gossip-sotomayor-deeply-closeted-lesbiancougar/.

12. Rebecca K. Lee, "Judging Judges: Empathy as the Litmus Test for Impartiality," *University of Cincinnati Law Review* 82 (2013), http://ssrn.com/abstract=2460626.

13. Robert Barnes and Paul Kane, "Sotomayor Repudiates 'Wise Latina' Comment: Cool amid Barrage by GOP senators," *Boston Globe,* July 15, 2009, http://www.boston.com/news/nation/washington/articles/2009/07/15/sotomayor_backs_off_wise_latina_quote/.

14. Emily Bazelon, "The Supreme Court's Painful Season," *New York Times,* August 5, 2011, http://www.nytimes.com/2011/08/07/magazine/the-supreme-courts-painful-season.html.

15. *Confirmation Hearing on the Nomination of Hon. Sonia Sotomayor, to Be an Associate Justice of the Supreme Court of the United States,* 111th Cong. 24–26 (2009) (statement of Hon. Charles Schumer, a U.S. Senator from New York), https://www.judiciary.senate.gov/imo/media/doc/GPO-CHRG-SOTOMAYOR.pdf.

16. Sotomayor's dissent centered on Pappas's First Amendment right to free speech. Pappas v. Giuliani, 290 F.3d 143 (2d Cir. 2002), https://caselaw.findlaw.com/us-2nd-circuit/1355900.html.

17. Ilan Stavans, Edna Acosta Belén, and Harold Augenbaum, introduction to *The Norton Anthology of Latino Literature,* ed. Ilan Stavans, Edna Acosta Belén, and Harold Augenbaum (New York: W. W. Norton, 2010), lxxl.

18. Mark Fenster, *Conspiracy Theories: Secrecy and Power in American Culture* (Minneapolis: University of Minnesota Press, 2008), 1.

19. Bloomberg Government, "Kavanaugh Hearing: Transcript," *Washington Post,* September 27, 2018, https://www.washingtonpost.com /news/national/wp/2018/09/27/kavanaugh-hearing-transcript/.

20. Adam Gabbat, "Anti-protest Bills Would 'Attack Right to Speak Out' under Donald Trump," *Guardian,* May 8, 2017, https://www .theguardian.com/world/2017/may/08/donald-trump-anti-protest-bills.

21. A second bomb sent to CNN was intercepted before it was delivered. Billionaire Democratic Party supporter George Soros also received a similar pipe bomb package. None of the bombs detonated.

22. Paul Glastris and Haley Sweetland Edwards, "The Big Lobotomy: How Republicans Made Congress Stupid," *Washington Monthly,* June–August 2014, https://washingtonmonthly.com/magazine/june-julyaug-2014/the-big-lobotomy/.

23. The CRS's Volunteer Internship Program still accepts "undergraduate students with exceptional academic talent." Last updated March 20, 2019, https://www.loc.gov/crsinfo/opportunities/volunteer .html.

24. Jeffery Gaynor, "The Contract with America: Implementing New Ideas in the U.S.," Heritage Foundation, October 12, 1995, https://www.heritage.org/political-process/report/the-contract-america-implementing-new-ideas-the-us.

25. Bruce Bartlett, "Gingrich and the Destruction of Congressional Expertise," *Economix* (blog), *New York Times,* November 29, 2011, https://economix.blogs.nytimes.com/2011/11/29/gingrich-and-the-destruction-of-congressional-expertise/.

26. For an early analysis of the goals of the Contract with America, see Major Garrett, "Beyond the Contract," *Mother Jones,* March/April 1995, https://www.motherjones.com/politics/1995/03/beyond-contract/.

27. "Stephen Miller Is the Architect of Family Separation at the Border. He Must Go," *Boston Globe,* June 20, 2018, https://www.bostonglobe .com/opinion/editorials/2018/06/19/stephen-miller-architect-family-separation-border-must/q7u4GAtQUdbrs1DSMgxoMI/story.html.

28. Clio2, "81 Infants and Children Seized at Border Have Been Found in Michigan," *Daily Kos,* June 20, 2018, https://www.dailykos

.com/stories/2018/6/20/1773703/-Eighty-One-Infants-and-Children-Seized-At-Border-Have-Been-Found-In-Michigan.

29. Rachel Black and Aleta Sprague, "The Rise and Reign of the Welfare Queen," *New America,* September 22, 2016, https://www.newamerica.org/weekly/edition-135/rise-and-reign-welfare-queen.

30. James Griffiths, "US Quits Human Rights Council: What Message Does It Send the World?," CNN, June 20, 2018, https://www.cnn.com/2018/06/20/politics/us-human-rights-council-intl/index.html.

31. Neal Devins and Lawrence Baum, "Split Definitive: How Party Polarization Turned the Supreme Court into a Partisan Court," *Supreme Court Review* 2016 (2016): 301–65, https://www.journals.uchicago.edu/doi/full/10.1086/691096.

32. Kyle Kim, "Trump Appointing Judges at Rapid Pace," *Los Angeles Times,* January, 19, 2018, http://www.latimes.com/projects/la-na-pol-trump-federal-judiciary/.

33. Michael Mitchell, Michael Leachman, and Kathleen Masterson, "A Lost Decade in Higher Education Funding: State Cuts Have Driven Up Tuition and Reduced Quality," Center on Budget and Policy Priorities, August 23, 2017, https://www.cbpp.org/research/state-budget-and-tax/a-lost-decade-in-higher-education-funding.

34. Ronald Brownstein, "American Higher Education Hits a Dangerous Milestone," *Atlantic,* May 3, 2018, https://www.theatlantic.com/politics/archive/2018/05/american-higher-education-hits-a-dangerous-milestone/559457/.

35. Ibid.

36. Jeremy Ashkenas, Haeyoun Park, and Adam Pearce, "Even with Affirmative Action, Blacks and Hispanics Are More Underrepresented at Top Colleges Than 35 Years Ago," *New York Times,* August 24, 2017, https://www.nytimes.com/interactive/2017/08/24/us/affirmative-action.html.

37. David Wiegel, "'Racialists' Are Cheered by Trump's Latest Strategy," *Washington Post,* August 20, 2016, https://www.washingtonpost.com/politics/racial-realists-are-cheered-by-trumps-latest-strategy/2016/08/20/cd71e858–6636–11e6–96c0–37533479f3f5.

CHAPTER FOUR. SONIA SOTOMAYOR AND OTHER STATES OF DEBT

1. Sonia Sotomayor, "Opening Statement to the Senate Judiciary Committee," *American Rhetoric: Online Speech Bank,* July 13, 2009, https://www.americanrhetoric.com/speeches/soniasotomayoropeningstmt.htm.

2. See Macarena Gómez-Barris's recent work on the incursions of "extractive capital" in the Americas: *Beyond the Pink Tide: Art and Political Undercurrents in the Americas* (Oakland: University of California Press, 2018), and *The Extractive Zone: Social Ecologies and Decolonial Perspectives* (Durham, NC: Duke University Press, 2017).

3. Antonia Felix, *Sonia Sotomayor: The True American Dream* (New York: Berkeley Books, 2010), 9.

4. See Patricia Gherovici, *The Puerto Rican Syndrome* (New York: Other Press, 2003), for a fascinating analysis of psychopathological affective patterns and hysteria attacks that afflicted Puerto Rican soldiers, whose reaction to war became known as the "Puerto Rican syndrome."

5. *WAC Handbook* (U.S. Army, 1944), Idelle Singletary Meng Scrapbook, Women Veterans Historical Project, University of North Carolina at Greensboro, http://libcdm1.uncg.edu/cdm/ref/collection/WVHP/id/9618.

6. My argument here is indebted to Laura Briggs's groundbreaking *Reproducing Empire: Race, Sex, Science, and U.S. Imperialism in Puerto Rico* (Berkeley: University for California Press, 2002).

7. See the Eugenics Archive online for "Puerto Rico": http://eugenicsarchive.ca/discover/tree/530ba18176fodb569booo01b.

8. Iris López, *Matters of Choice: Puerto Rican Women's Struggle for Reproductive Freedom* (New Brunswick, NJ: Rutgers University Press, 2008), ii–xxiv.

9. "Induction Proceedings for Judge Sonia Sotomayor," November 6, 1998, p. 31, https://judicial-discipline-reform.org/SCt_nominee/98–11–6JSotomayor_induction_proceedings.pdf.

10. El Museo del Barrio's exhibit "Nueva York (1613–1945)" ran from September 7, 2010, to January 9, 2011.

11. Ramón Bosque-Pérez, "Political Persecution against Puerto Rican Anti-colonial Activists in the Twentieth-Century," in *Puerto*

Rico under Colonial Rule: Political Persecution and the Quest for Human Rights, ed. Ramón Bosque-Pérez and José Javier Colón Morera (Albany, NY: SUNY University Press, 2006), 28–29.

12. Susan E. Lederer, "'Porto Ricochet': Joking about Germs, Cancer, and Race Extermination in the 1930s," *American Literary History* 14, no. 4 (Winter 2002): 720–46.

13. Ibid.

14. Ibid., 772.

15. Jonathan Eig, "A San Juan Weekend," chap. 17 in *How Four Crusaders Reinvented Sex and Launched a Revolution* (New York: W.W. Norton, 2014).

16. On the incidence of premature puberty in Puerto Rico, see Ora H. Pescovitz and Emily C. Walvoord, "Endocrine Disruptors in Puberty," chap. 20 in *When Puberty Is Precocious: Scientific and Clinical Aspects* (Totowa, NJ: Humana Press, 2007). On the incidence of "indeterminate" sex differentiation in Puerto Rico, see C. Gulledge, "Endocrine Disruption in Sexual Differentiation and Puberty: What Do Pseudohermaphroditic Polar Bears Have to Do with the Practice of Pediatrics?," *Pediatric Clinics of North America* 48, no. 5 (2001): 1223–40.

17. Dolores "Lolita" Lebrón Sotomayor, *Sándalo en la celda* (San Juan, PR: Editorial Betances, 1975).

18. Elyse Wanshel, "Sonia Sotomayor Sends a Message to Puerto Rico: 'You Are Not Alone,'" *Huffington Post,* September 28, 2017, https://www.huffingtonpost.com/entry/sonia-sotomayor-sends-powerful-message-of-hope-to-residents-of-puerto-rico_us_59cd14ede4b0e005cc572acd.

19. David A. Graham, "Trump's Dubious Revisionist History of Hurricane Maria," *Atlantic,* September 12, 2018, https://www.theatlantic.com/politics/archive/2018/09/trump-hurricane-maria-florence-revisionism/570070/.

CODA

1. For a concise review of these and other interpretive positions, see Brandon J. Murrill, "Modes of Constitutional Interpretation,"

Congressional Research Service, March 2018, https://fas.org/sgp/crs/misc/R45129.pdf.

2. Jean Stefancic, "Latino and Latina Critical Theory: An Annotated Bibliography," *California Law Review* 85, no. 5 (October 1997): 1512, https://scholarship.law.berkeley.edu/cgi/viewcontent.cgi?article=1611&context=californialawreview.

3. Ibid., 1512.

4. Francisco Valdes, "Legal Reform and Social Justice: An Introduction to LatCrit Theory, Praxis and Community," *Griffith Law Review* 14, no. 2 (2005): 148–49, http://latcrit.org/media/medialibrary/2014/02/142_3_valdes.pdf.

5. Ibid.

6. David A. Kaplan, *The Most Dangerous Branch: Inside the Supreme Court's Assault on the Constitution* (New York: Crown, 2018), 123 passim.

7. José Esteban Muñoz, "Wise Latinas," *Criticism* 56, no. 2 (Spring 2014): 249.

8. Citizens United v. Federal Election Comm'n, 558 U.S. 310 (2010), https://supreme.justia.com/cases/federal/us/558/310/.

9. Michigan v. Bryant, 562 U.S. 344 (2011), https://supreme.justia.com/cases/federal/us/562/344/.

10. Masterpiece Cakeshop, Ltd. v. Colorado Civil Rights Commission, 584 U.S. ____ (2018), https://supreme.justia.com/cases/federal/us/584/16-111/.

11. International Justice Resource Center, "Requiring Operation to Correct Sex on Birth Certificate Violates Rights," April 18, 2017, https://ijrcenter.org/2017/04/18/requiring-operation-to-correct-sex-on-birth-certificate-violates-rights/; Liam Stack, "European Court Strikes Down Required Sterilization for Transgender People," *New York Times,* April 12, 2017, https://www.nytimes.com/2017/04/12/world/europe/european-court-strikes-down-required-sterilization-for-transgender-people.html.

12. Times Editorial Board, "A Baker Can't Discriminate in the Name of Free Speech or Religion," *Los Angeles Times,* December 6, 2017, https://www.latimes.com/opinion/editorials/la-ed-scotus-cake-20171206-story.html.

13. Fisher v. University of Texas at Austin, 579 U.S. ____ (2016), https://supreme.justia.com/cases/federal/us/579/14–981/.

14. Elena Kagan recused herself due to her prior involvement in the case as solicitor general for the Obama administration.

15. Parents Involved in Community Schools v. Seattle School Dist. No. 1, 551 U.S. 701 (2007), https://supreme.justia.com/cases/federal/us/551/701/.

16. Schuette v. Coal. Defend Affirmative Action, Integration & Immigration Rights, 572 U.S. ____ (2014), https://supreme.justia.com/cases/federal/us/572/12–682/.

17. Walter Benjamin, "The Work of Art in the Age of Its Technological Reproducibility, Second Version," in *The Work of Art in the Age of Its Technological Reproducibility, and Other Writings on Media,* ed. Michael W. Jennings, Brigid Doherty, and Thomas Y. Levin (Cambridge, MA: Harvard University Press, 2008), 41.

18. Under the "Three-Fifths Compromise" of the Constitution, all slaves were to be counted as three-fifths of a white man. The Thirteenth Amendment to the U.S. Constitution, enacted after the Civil War, rendered the "Three-Fifths Compromise" obsolete though its legacies live on well into our present.

SELECTED BIBLIOGRAPHY

Baty, S. Paige. *American Monroe: The Making of a Body Politic.* Berkeley: University of California Press, 1995.

Berlant, Lauren. *Cruel Optimism.* Durham, NC: Duke University Press, 2011.

Bonilla-Silva, Eduardo. *Racism without Racists: Color-Blind Racism and the Persistence of Racial Inequality in America.* Lanham, MD: Rowman and Littlefield, 2013.

Boston Globe. "Stephen Miller Is the Architect of Family Separation at the Border. He Must Go." June 20, 2018. https://www.bostonglobe.com/opinion/editorials/2018/06/19/stephen-miller-architect-family-separation-border-must/q7u4GAtQUdbrs1DSMgx0MI/story.html.

Briggs, Laura. *Reproducing Empire: Race, Sex, Science, and U.S. Imperialism in Puerto Rico.* Berkeley: University for California Press, 2002.

Carnevale, Anthony P., and Jeff Strohl. *Separate and Unequal: How Higher Education Reinforces the Intergenerational Reproduction of White Racial Privilege.* Washington, DC: Georgetown Public Policy Institute, 2013. http://cew.georgetown.edu/separateandunequal/.

Chambers-Letson, Joshua. "Embodying Justice: The Making of Justice Sonia Sotomayor." *Women and Performance: A Journal of Feminist Theory* 20, no. 2 (July 2010): 149–72.

Chávez, Leo R. *The Latino Threat: Constructing Immigrants, Citizens, and the Nation.* 2nd ed. Stanford, CA: Stanford University Press, 2013 [2008].

Chivvis, Dana. "Arizona Outlaws Mexican-American Studies Program." *AOL News/Huffington Post,* January 10, 2011. http://www.aolnews.com/2011/01/10/arizona-outlaws-mexican-american-studies-program/.

Cho, Sumi. "Post-racialism." *Iowa Law Review* 94 (2009): 1589–649.

Du Bois, W. E. B. *The Souls of Black Folk.* Edited by Brent Hayes Edwards. New York: Oxford University Press, 2007 [1903].

Eig, Jonathan. *How Four Crusaders Reinvented Sex and Launched a Revolution.* New York: W. W. Norton, 2014.

Emerson, Ralph Waldo. *Representative Men.* New York: Library of America, 1983 [1850].

Fenster, Mark. *Conspiracy Theories: Secrecy and Power in American Culture.* Minneapolis: University of Minnesota Press, 2008.

Gándara, Patricia, and Frances Contreras. *The Latino Education Crisis: The Consequences of Failed Social Policies.* Cambridge, MA: Harvard University Press, 2009.

Gómez-Barris, Macarena. *Beyond the Pink Tide: Art and Political Undercurrents in the Americas.* Oakland: University of California Press, 2018.

———. *The Extractive Zone: Social Ecologies and Decolonial Perspectives.* Durham, NC: Duke University Press, 2017.

Graham, David A. "Trump's Dubious Revisionist History of Hurricane Maria." *Atlantic,* September 12, 2018. https://www.theatlantic.com/politics/archive/2018/09/trump-hurricane-maria-florence-revisionism/570070/.

Guinier, Lani, and Gerald Torres. *The Miner's Canary: Enlisting Race, Resisting Power, Transforming Democracy.* Cambridge, MA: Harvard University Press, 2003.

Hernstein, Richard J., and Charles Murray. *The Bell Curve: Intelligence and Class Structure in American Life.* New York: Free Press, 1994.

Higginbothom, F. Michael. *Ghosts of Jim Crow: Ending Racism in Post-racial America.* New York: NYU Press, 2013.

Hochschild, Jennifer L. *The American Dream and the Public Schools*. New York: Oxford University Press, 2003.

Jefferies, Michael P. *Paint the White House Black: Barack Obama and the Meaning of Race in America*. Palo Alto, CA: Stanford University Press, 2013.

Kaplan, David A. *The Most Dangerous Branch: Inside the Supreme Court's Assault on the Constitution*. New York: Crown, 2018.

Katznelson, Ira. *When Affirmative Action Was White: An Untold History of Racial Inequality in Twentieth-Century America*. New York: W. W. Norton, 2005.

Kim, Kyle. "Trump Appointing Judges at Rapid Pace." *Los Angeles Times,* January 18, 2018. http://www.latimes.com/projects/la-na-pol-trump-federal-judiciary/.

Lebrón Sotomayor, Dolores. *Sándalo en la celda*. San Juan, PR: Editorial Betances, 1975.

Lederer, Susan E. "'Porto Ricochet': Joking about Germs, Cancer, and Race Extermination in the 1930s." *American Literary History* 14, no. 4 (Winter 2002): 720–746.

Lilley, Sandra. "Poll: 1 out of 3 Americans Inaccurately Think Most Hispanics Are Undocumented." NBC Latino, September 9, 2012. http://nbclatino.com/2012/09/12/poll-1-out-of-3-americans-think-most-hispanics-are-undocumented/.

Lima, Lázaro. *The Latino Body: Crisis Identities in American Literary and Cultural Memory*. New York: NYU Press, 2007.

———. "Spanish Speakers and Early Latino Expression." In *American History through Literature, 1820–1870*, vol. 3, edited by Janet Gabler-Hover and Robert Sattelmeyer, 1118–23. New York: Charles Scribner's and Sons, 2006.

Mack, Kenneth W. Mack. *Representing the Race: The Creation of the Civil Rights Lawyer*. Cambridge, MA: Harvard University Press, 2012.

Marrero, Pilar. *Killing the American Dream: How Anti-immigration Extremists Are Destroying the Nation*. New York: Palgrave-Macmillan, 2012.

McKinley, James, Jr. "Texas Conservatives Win Curriculum Change." *New York Times,* March 12, 2010. http://www.nytimes.com/2010/03/13/education/13texas.html.

Mettler, Suzanne. *Degrees of Inequality: How the Politics of Higher Education Sabotaged the American Dream.* New York: Basic Books, 2014.

Milian, Claudia. *Latining America: Black-Brown Passages and the Coloring of Latino/a Studies.* Athens: University of Georgia Press, 2013.

Muñoz, José Esteban. "Feeling Brown, Feeling Down: Latina Affect, the Performativity of Race, and the Depressive Position." *Signs* 31, no. 3 (Spring 2006): 675–88.

———. "Preface: Fragment from the *Sense of Brown* Manuscript." In "The Queer Commons," by Nadja Millner-Larsen and Gavin Butt, *GLQ* 24, no. 4 (2018): 395–97.

———. "Wise Latinas." *Criticism* 56, no. 2 (Spring 2014): 249–65.

Murray, Charles. "In Defense of Jason Richwine." *National Review,* May,15,2013.http://www.nationalreview.com/article/348323/defense-jason-richwine.

Negrón-Muntaner, Frances. "Confirmed: Sonia Sotomayor and the Limits of Latino Political Incorporation." *Journal of Transnational American Studies* 3, no. 2 (2011). https://escholarship.org/uc/item/4nb9249f.

Negrón-Muntaner, Frances, et al. *The Latino Media Gap: A Report on the State of Latinos in the U.S. Media.* New York: Center for the Study of Race and Ethnicity, Columbia University, 2014.

Newfield, Christopher. *Unmaking the Public University: The Forty-Year Assault on the Middle Class.* Cambridge, MA: Harvard University Press, 2008.

Nyong'o, Tavia. "Barack Hussein Obama, or, The Name of the Father." *Scholar and Feminist Online,* no. 7.2 (Spring 2009). http://sfonline.barnard.edu/africana/nyongo_01.htm.

Olivas, Michael A. *Colored Men and Hombres Aquí: Hernández v. Texas and the Emergence of Mexican American Lawyering.* Houston: Arte Público Press, 2006.

Perry, Imani. *More Beautiful and More Terrible: The Embrace and Transcendence of Racial Inequality in the United States.* New York: NYU Press, 2011.

Ransby, Barbara. *Making All Black Lives Matter: Reimagining Freedom in the 21st Century.* Oakland: University of California Press, 2018.

Rector, Robert, and Jason Richwine. "The Fiscal Cost of Unlawful Immigrants and Amnesty to the U.S. Taxpayer." Heritage Foundation, May

6, 2013. https://www.heritage.org/immigration/report/the-fiscal-cost-unlawful-immigrants-and-amnesty-the-us-taxpayer.

Rosen, Jeffrey. "The Case against Sotomayor." *New Republic,* May 4, 2009.http://www.newrepublic.com/article/politics/the-case-against-sotomayor?id=45d56e6f-f497-4b19-9c63-04e10199a085.

Schumer, Charles. *Confirmation Hearing on the Nomination Of Hon. Sonia Sotomayor, to Be an Associate Justice of the Supreme Court of the United States,* 111th Cong. 24–26 (2009) (statement of Hon. Charles Schumer, a U.S. Senator from New York). https://www.judiciary.senate.gov/imo/media/doc/GPO-CHRG-SOTOMAYOR.pdf.

Smith, Hedrick. *Who Stole the American Dream?* New York: Random House, 2012.

Stefancic, Jean, and Richard Delgado. *No Mercy: How Conservative Think Tanks and Foundations Changed America's Social Agenda.* Philadelphia: Temple University Press, 1996.

Wanshel, Elyse. "Sonia Sotomayor Sends a Message to Puerto Rico: 'You Are Not Alone.'" *Huffington Post,* September 28, 2017. https://www.huffingtonpost.com/entry/sonia-sotomayor-sends powerful-message-of-hope-to-residents-of-puerto-rico_us_59cd14ede4boeoo5cc572acd.

Wise, Tim. *Colorblind: The Rise of Post-racial Politics and the Retreat from Racial Equity.* San Francisco: City Lights, 2010.

Zakaria, Rafia. "How Trump Is Stripping Immigrants of Their Citizenship." *Nation,* December 21, 2018. https://www.thenation.com/article/denaturalization-trump-citizenship-emma-goldman/.

Founded in 1893,
UNIVERSITY OF CALIFORNIA PRESS
publishes bold, progressive books and journals
on topics in the arts, humanities, social sciences,
and natural sciences—with a focus on social
justice issues—that inspire thought and action
among readers worldwide.

The UC PRESS FOUNDATION
raises funds to uphold the press's vital role
as an independent, nonprofit publisher, and
receives philanthropic support from a wide
range of individuals and institutions—and from
committed readers like you. To learn more, visit
ucpress.edu/supportus.